December 1989

Helen,

Have an e,
Christmas this year.

Love
Bev, Jarvis,
Adrienne & Heather

The Heritage Book 1990

Edna McCann

Collier Macmillan Canada, Inc.

Collier Macmillan Canada, Inc.
1200 Eglinton Ave. East, Suite 200
Don Mills, Ontario   M3C 3N1

ISBN 02.953911.0

Printed and bound in Canada

Fourteenth Edition

PICTURE CREDITS

Today we stand at the threshold of a new decade—the last of the twentieth century. How strange it is to be living at the beginning of a whole new era!

Although it is with awe and excitement that we contemplate the future, our thoughts inevitably turn to the welfare of future generations. How will our great-grandchildren fare in the years to come? Will they still delight in the fragrance of the daffodil, and thrill to the song of spring's first robin?

Yet in all the uncertainty of our age, we have only to remember the strength of our eternal values. From these we draw our hope and inspiration—the love of family, the spirit of faith, and the common humanity that compels us to reach out to others.

Throughout this exciting time, I hope that you will find this little book to be a comforting and inspiring companion. May you have many joyful and fulfilling days in the year to come.

Edna McCann

January

TODAY marks the beginning, not only of a new year, but also of a new decade.

I believe this prayer, written by Reinhold Niebuhr, gives good advice to us all as we enter the last decade of the twentieth century.

O God, give us serenity to accept what cannot be changed, courage to change what should be changed, and wisdom to distinguish the one from the other.

TUESDAY — JANUARY 2

IT's nice after the hectic pace of the last few weeks to spend some quiet time alone. So it was with great pleasure today that I set a fire in the fireplace and sat down in my favourite chair to read one of the many new books that I received as Christmas gifts.

Although I read all types of books with great pleasure, many of my favourites are either mysteries or stories written by humourists.

I found myself laughing out loud today as I read and by this evening I realized how much better I felt.

There must be a lot of truth to the old expression, "Laughter is the best medicine."

WEDNESDAY — JANUARY 3

WHENEVER you are to do a thing, though it can never be known but to yourself, ask yourself how you would act were all the world looking at you, and act accordingly.

—Thomas Jefferson

THE HERITAGE BOOK

My friend Jake Frampton stopped by for dinner this evening. Our friendship goes back so many years that it is more like having a family member for dinner than having "company."

Jake comes by quite regularly to share a meal. Since his wife passed away many years ago Jake has found mealtimes alone very difficult. We discussed this problem over our dinner.

"You know, Edna, I'm sure that many people who live alone find this to be as much of a problem as I do. It is certainly not enjoyable to cook for one person, nor do I find eating alone a pleasant experience. Often I will skip a meal altogether rather than go to the bother of cooking for myself."

On occasions when I eat alone I often turn on my television for company. Just the sound of people speaking in the room seems to alleviate the feeling of loneliness.

My friend Barbara has an unusual solution. She often takes her dinner on a tray to the laundry room of her apartment building where, as she says, there is almost always someone doing their wash. "I enjoy the company and so do they."

Friday — January 5

As I am well aware, one can never know everything there is to be known about human nature. One can be sure only of one thing, and that is that it will never cease to have a surprise in store for you.

—*W. Somerset Maugham*

Saturday — January 6

Today is the celebration of the Epiphany, the twelfth day after Christmas. For many of our European friends this is the day that the birth of Jesus is celebrated. One of my favourite carols for this day is "O Come All Ye Faithful."

O come all ye faithful, joyful and triumphant;
O come ye, O come ye to Bethlehem.
Come and behold Him, born the King of
    Angels;
O come, let us adore Him, O come let us adore
    Him
O come let us adore Him, Christ the Lord.

SUNDAY — JANUARY 7

LORD, keep my parents in your love.
Lord, bless them and keep them.
Lord, please let me have money and strength
    and keep my parents for many years
So that I can take care of them.
Amen.
—The Prayer of a young Ghanian Christian

MONDAY — JANUARY 8

MY granddaughter, Phyllis, paid us a visit on the weekend. She and her husband Bill brought along their four-year-old twins, Justin and Jenny. It was a delightful time for all of us.

The twins are at an interesting age. On the one hand, they are trying to act "grown up" by sitting quietly and talking about all the exciting things they are doing in "real" school (junior nursery). On the other hand, they still race for Grampa's knee when my son-in-law Bruce offers to read them a story at bedtime.

Justin echoed a sentiment that perhaps all of us have experienced. "Gee, Grampa, I hope I never get too big to sit on your lap. It's sure comfortable."

THE HERITAGE BOOK

I enjoy the work of Emily Dickinson. This poem, entitled "The Snow," is one of my favourites.

It sifts from Leaden Sieves—
It powders all the Field—
It fills with Alabaster Wool
The Wrinkles of the Road—

It makes an even face
Of Mountain—and of Plain—
Unbroken Forehead from the East
Unto the East—again—

It reaches to the Fence—
It wraps it, Rail by Rail,
Till it is lost in Fleeces—
It flings a Crystal Vail

On Stump—and Stack—and Stem—
The Summers empty Room—
Acres of Joints—where Harvests were—
Recordless—but for them—

It Ruffles Wrists of Posts—
As Ancles of a Queen—
Then stills it's Artisans—like Swans—
Denying they have been—

THE HERITAGE BOOK

<u>WEDNESDAY — JANUARY 10</u>

THERE are many stories today of families with multiple births. With the advent of fertility drugs, quadruplets, quintuplets, and even sextuplets have become almost a common event.

But back in 1934, at the time of the Dionne quintuplets' birth, it was such a rarity that people flocked by the thousands to the tiny town of Corbeil, Ontario, to catch a glimpse of the five celebrated little girls.

Twice a day crowds of people would gather to watch Annette, Marie, Cécile, Emilie, and Yvonne at play. Although the girls were behind a one-way screen, they were well aware of the many people who watched.

Once, one quint held up a monkey-faced doll. One of her sisters chastised her by saying, "Put that away or they will think we are six!"

<u>THURSDAY — JANUARY 11</u>

YOU needn't tell people what you know—they can tell by the things you do.

FRIDAY — JANUARY 12

IN most undertakings success requires not only initiative, but also finishiative.

SATURDAY — JANUARY 13

MY son-in-law John, who is a minister, was much amused by the following anecdote.

Many years ago in the west a minister stopped to preach at an Indian reservation. Before leaving for the prayer meeting he asked his host, the Indian Chief, if he could safely leave his belongings in his teepee.

"Certainly," replied the chief, "there isn't a white man within fifty miles."

SUNDAY — JANUARY 14

GOD, of your goodness give me yourself, for you are sufficient for me. I cannot properly ask anything less, to be worthy of you. If I should ask less I should always be in want. In you alone do I have all.

—*Julien of Norwich*

MONDAY — JANUARY 15

MY good friend Mavis Tewbury wrote to me in great excitement. Later this year she will become a great-grandmother for the first time.

"Because this is so special to me I wanted to do something unique for the coming baby. A friend of mine gave me the perfect idea, Edna. I have started a scrapbook of this year's events. I am filling the pages with interesting headlines and news stories. As well, I am putting in fashion photos, food and movie advertisements, and pictures of cars and famous people. I have collected "top ten" music charts and photos of the whole family as they look this year.

"The last page of the book will be saved for the announcement of the baby's birth and a picture."

I can't think of any better way to welcome a new grandchild.

TUESDAY — JANUARY 16

FAITH is the opening of all sides and every level of one's life to the divine overflow.
                          —*Martin Luther King Jr.*

THE HERITAGE BOOK

WEDNESDAY — JANUARY 17

THE most evident sign of wisdom is continued cheerfulness.
                                              —*Michel de Montaigne*

THURSDAY — JANUARY 18

To be needed in other human lives—is there anything greater or more beautiful in this world.
                                              —*David Grayson*

FRIDAY — JANUARY 19

IN times of quietness our hearts should be like trees, lifting their branches to the sky to draw down strength which they will need to face the storms that will surely come.
                                              —*Toyohiko Kagawa*

SATURDAY — JANUARY 20

THE true test of civilization is, not the census, nor the size of cities, nor the crops— no, but the kind of man the country turns out.
                                              —*Ralph Waldo Emerson*

SUNDAY — JANUARY 21

THE heavens declare the glory of God, and his firmament shouteth his handiwork. One day telleth another, and one night certifieth another. There is neither speech nor language, their voices cannot be heard. Yet their sound is gone out into all lands; and their words into the end of the world.

—Psalm 19:1-4

MONDAY — JANUARY 22

DURING the extremely cold weather at this time of year there are many different suggestions about how to keep warm without racking up staggering utilities bills.

Thermal underwear, unlike the old thick and itchy "long-johns," is thin, easily worn under clothing, and extremely warm. In bed, the good old flannel sheet is a warm comfort, as is a hot water bottle for the feet (for those who don't care for the electric blanket).

Eating well can also keep you warm. Something hot for breakfast as well as warm drinks throughout the day keep the chill away.

Or, as my good friend Emily writes, "Come to Florida!" A nice idea, too.

TUESDAY — JANUARY 23

My granddaughter Phyllis' closest friend Christie is a schoolteacher. One of the chores that Christie finds most difficult is writing report cards that are encouraging, fair, and give parents a clear picture of how their son or daughter is progressing.

This semester, Christie's principal gave each teacher a copy of a report card sent home from a school in the U.S., along with the parent's reply. The source was unknown but it gave several teachers a hearty chuckle.

"Our school's cross-graded, multi-ethnic, individualized learning program is designed to enhance the concept of an open-ended learning program with emphasis on a continuum of multi-ethnic academically enriched learning, using the identified intellectually gifted child as the agent or director of his own learning. Major emphasis is on cross-graded, multi-ethnic learning with the main objective being to learn respect for the uniqueness of a person."

The father wrote back, "I have a college degree, speak two foreign languages and four Indian dialects. I have talked with diplomats, foreign heads of state, and one king, but I haven't the faintest idea what you're talking about."

WEDNESDAY — JANUARY 24

IT is better to light one small candle than to curse the darkness.

—Confucius

THURSDAY — JANUARY 25

When You Are Old

WHEN you are old and gray and full of
    sleep,
And nodding by the fire, take down this book,
And slowly read, and dream of the soft look
Your eyes had once, and of their shadows
    deep;

How many loved your moments of glad grace,
And loved your beauty with love false or true;
But one man loved the pilgrim soul in you,
And loved the sorrows of your changing face.

And bending down beside the glowing bars,
Murmur, a little sadly, how love fled
And paced upon the mountains overhead
And hid his face amid a crowd of stars.

—William Butler Yeats

FRIDAY — JANUARY 26

MAKE a rule, and pray God, to help you keep it, never, if possible, to lie down at night without being able to say, "I have made one human being, at least, a little wiser, a little happier, or a little better this day."

—*Charles Kingsley*

SATURDAY — JANUARY 27

TONIGHT'S hockey game brought to mind a story about one of the game's great players.

The Depression winter of 1932 was a tough one for all of Canada, and no less so for Saskatoon, where Albert and Katherine Howe were hard-pressed to feed their young family. But when a young mother came to their door with a sackful of odds and ends to sell Katherine gave her $1.50 so that the mother could buy milk for her baby.

When she emptied the bag a pair of small children's skates fell out. "Mine!" said her four-year-old son. "No, mine!" cried his three-year-old sister Edna. They put on one skate each and went out to slide on the ice behind their home. After a week Edna sold her share of the skates for a dime and Gordie Howe had started his climb to the N.H.L.

SUNDAY — JANUARY 28

Aʜ, dearest Jesus, holy Child;
Make thee a bed, soft, undefiled,
Within my heart, that it may be
A quiet chamber, kept for thee.
—*Martin Luther*

MONDAY — JANUARY 29

My sister Sarah surprised me with a phone call this evening. Sarah lives on the east coast, and although we correspond regularly she is not one who uses the telephone indiscriminately. So it was with concern that I asked if all was well.

"Yes, Edna, everything is just fine—I just missed hearing your voice."

We talked for a long time about the family and old friends. It was as if we were young girls again, lying in our beds at night and talking about school chums and our beaux. Finally we both said our reluctant goodbyes.

After I hung up I realized how lucky I am to have a sister who loves me enough to call for no special reason.

TUESDAY — JANUARY 30

HE is rich who owns the day, and no one owns the day who allows it to be invaded by worry, fret and anxiety.

—Ralph Waldo Emerson

WEDNESDAY — JANUARY 31

WHEN the winter evenings lengthen
And the daily chores are done,
Then we gather round the fireside
For a bit of family fun.

Logs of apple wood lie burning
In the fireplace, embers bright,
Heaps of popcorn slowly dribble
From the spider, gleaming white.

Fun and laughter, games and music
Echo through each room and hall;
Winter evening's time for playing.
We left care with passing fall.

Let the moonbeams cast their shadows
On the snow clad earth tonight,
We will bind our family closer
By the cozy fireplace light.

—Elva Weber

February

ONE of the new year's resolutions that I made this year was in the form of a promise to Marg and Bruce. I resolved that I would go through some of my many boxes of books with a view to discarding those I no longer need or use.

It has been a wonderful experience. I feel as if I have discovered some "old friends" in these boxes—historical novels, epic poems, and many a Victorian romance—all classics in their times. It was very difficult to decide which of these books to keep and which to discard. I finally chose the ones that evoked the most pleasant memories and packed up the rest.

Bruce took the boxes to our local nursing home. I hope they will give some of the residents there a few hours of pleasure.

This evening I will read some of these long-forgotten stories and remember.

THE HERITAGE BOOK

Friday — February 2

THIS is a day that I always enjoy very much. It is the one day in the year when we "conservative" Canadians feel free to be just a little silly. After all, how often do people rely on a groundhog to predict the coming weather?

I particularly enjoyed this evening's television news and weather. The weather forecaster, dapper in his sports jacket, shirt and tie, announced with a very straight face that "since Wiarton Willie, our groundhog, emerged today from his hole and saw his shadow, we can look forward to six more weeks of winter."

With all of our technological advances, weather satellites, and the like, I somehow feel that our little animal predictor will again turn out to be the most accurate.

Saturday — February 3

THERE is in every true woman's heart a spark of heavenly fire, which lies dormant in the broad daylight of prosperity, but which kindles up and beams and blazes in the dark hour of adversity.

—*Washington Irving*

THE HERITAGE BOOK

SUNDAY — FEBRUARY 4

IT happened at this time that Jesus came down from Nazareth in Galilee and was baptized in the Jordan by John. At that moment, when he came up out of the water he saw the heavens torn open and the Spirit, like a dove, descending upon him. And a voice spoke from heaven, "Thou art my Son, my beloved; on thee my favour rests."

—Mark 1: 9-11

MONDAY — FEBRUARY 5

THERE is a vast difference between putting your nose in other people's business and putting your heart in other people's problems.

TUESDAY — FEBRUARY 6

YOUTH is happy because it has the ability to see beauty. Anyone who keeps the ability to see beauty never grows old.

—Franz Kafka

THE HERITAGE BOOK

As I was reading this morning I came across an ancient Blackfoot Indian prayer, which speaks to us all.

O Great Spirit, Creator of all things;
Human beings, trees, grass, berries.
Help us, be kind to us,
Let us be happy on earth.
Let us lead our children
To a good life and old age.
These our people; give them good minds
To love one another.

O Great Spirit,
Be kind to us.
Give these people the favour
To see green trees,
Green grass, flowers and berries
This next spring;
So we all meet again.

O Great Spirit,
We ask of You.

THE HERITAGE BOOK

SEVERAL years ago I went to one of the loveliest funerals I have ever attended. How can a funeral be "lovely," you might ask. Let me explain.

Jane Kuhn was a good friend and teaching colleague of my granddaughter Phyllis. She and her husband Jim had one son, Trevor. Two years before her death Jane found out that she had cancer. She went on to endure an operation and many types of treatments. The drug therapy would often make her deathly sick, and she also lost her hair. And yet through it all she was uncomplaining and hopeful.

Eventually it became clear that a cure was not to be. Jane became weaker and eventually bedridden. When she realized she would soon be leaving her earthly body Jane decided to plan her own funeral. She gathered together her closest friends and asked each of them to share in the service with a Scripture reading, a poem, or by sharing Jane's affirmations of the life she felt she was to begin in the Spiritual Kingdom.

Phyllis and I came away from Jane's funeral feeling both grief at the loss of a wonderful person, and joy in her faith in the life hereafter.

Friday — February 9

'Tis a maxim with me to be young as long as one can; there is nothing one can pay for that invaluable ignorance which is the companion of youth; those sanguine groundless hopes, and that lively vanity, which makes all the happiness of life. To my extreme mortification I grow wiser every day.

Saturday — February 10

My grandson Fred, his wife June, and their two sons Micky and Geoffrey hosted a "winter carnival" today at their country home. Friends, neighbours, and relatives participated enthusiastically in such events as toboggan racing, three-legged snowshoeing, and ski relay races.

Those of us who were in the "cheering section" kept warm beside a roaring fire. Hot chocolate and mulled cider steamed in large pots and hotdogs and hamburgers kept up the energy level of the competitors.

By evening all of us were tired, but happy to have spent a day enjoying good fun and company in what can be a long winter.

THE HERITAGE BOOK

ALMIGHTY God, who at the baptism of thy blessed son Jesus Christ in the river Jordan dids't manifest his glorious Godhead, grant we beseech thee, that the brightness of His presence may shine in our hearts, and His glory be set forth in our lives; through the same Jesus Christ our Lord.

—Epiphany - Scottish Prayer Book

MONDAY — FEBRUARY 12

A man that I greatly admired was Jules Leger, a diplomat, scholar, and former Governor General of Canada. M. Leger was born in St. Anicet, Québec, on April 4, 1913. From 1933-36 he studied law at the University of Montréal. After a two-year doctorate at the Sorbonne he married Gabrielle Carmel. They had two daughters, Francine and Hélène.

A few of the positions held by M. Leger include Professor, University of Ottawa; Secretary, Canadian Embassy, Chile; Assistant to Prime Minister Louis St. Laurent; Under-Secretary of State for External Affairs; and, of course, Canadian Governor General.

Tuesday — February 13

LIFE is like a coin—you can spend it any way you wish but you can spend it only once.

Wednesday — February 14

FOR this Valentine's Day I offer you Sara Teasdale's poem entitled "Song."

You bound strong sandals on my feet
You gave me bread and wine,
And sent me under sun and stars,
For all the world was mine.

Oh take the sandals off my feet,
You know not what you do;
For all my world is in your arms,
My sun and stars are you.

Thursday — February 15

NOTHING really makes the younger generation seem so bad as having lost your membership in it.

As I grow older I value more and more the friendships I have been fortunate enough to develop over these many years. Numerous people have expressed their ideas of friendship and here are but a few.

Life is nothing without friendship.

—Cicero

Be courteous to all, but intimate with few, and let those few be well tried before you give them your confidence. True friendship is a plant of slow growth, and must undergo and withstand the shocks of adversity before it is entitled to the appellation.

—George Washington

A true friend is the greatest of all blessings.
—Duc de la Rochefoucauld

Friendship is the marriage of the soul.

—Voltaire

A friend is a present which you give yourself.
—Robert Louis Stevenson

SATURDAY — FEBRUARY 17

ALL of us want to be good Samaritans when loved ones are confined in the hospital, but often our visits may be "bad medicine" for seriously ill patients. If you've ever been a hospital patient you'll appreciate these suggestions made by physicians, nurses, and hospital executives.

Remember to limit the time that you stay. People who have been ill are weak and tire easily. Fifteen minutes is the time suggested by many doctors. If the patient has had other company ten minutes is plenty.

If the patient wants to talk about his or her illness be a good listener, but don't start that conversation. To give someone a lift, talk about their tennis game, or how much you've enjoyed a party with them, or bring news of friends. In an effort to be cheerful many of us raise our voices. Keep your voice down—don't yell. Thoughtful gifts include puzzles, card decks, and magazines.

If a doctor believes that many visitors, phone calls, etc. will help morale, he or she will tell the patient's family. A safe rule to follow is: Never visit anyone who is sick unless you are a close relative or a close friend.

Good advice for all of us.

THE HERITAGE BOOK

A mighty fortress is our God
A bulwark never failing,
Our helper He amid the flood
Of mortal ills prevailing.

—Martin Luther

GIVE me work to do;
Give me health;
Give me joy in simple things.
Give me an eye for beauty,
A tongue for truth,
A heart that loves,
A mind that reasons,
A sympathy that understands;
Give me neither malice nor envy,
But a true kindness
And a noble common sense.
At the close of each day
Give me a book,
And a friend with whom
I can be silent.

THE HERITAGE BOOK

TUESDAY — FEBRUARY 20

I went to the woods because I wished to live deliberately, to confront only the essential facts of life, and see if I could not learn what it had to teach, and not when I come to die, discover that I had not lived.

—*Henry David Thoreau*

WEDNESDAY — FEBRUARY 21

FOR many years my brother Ben and his wife Marie lived on a farm. During that time they never once locked the doors. This used to amaze friends and relatives who came to visit from the city.

"Well, for gracious' sake," Marie used to say, "if we locked them how could the neighbours get in to see if everything is all right?"

THURSDAY — FEBRUARY 22

THE creation of a thousand forests is in one acorn.

—*Ralph Waldo Emerson*

MY husband George always enjoyed bits of Canadian folklore. This is a story I think he would have liked.

In 1903 the only population centres in northeastern Ontario were New Liskeard and Haileybury. But the area was the scene of much activity, as the Temiskaming and Northern Ontario Railway was being built to join North Bay and New Liskeard. The railway would open up timbering and farming possibilities for the whole area. As it happened, the railway would do much more.

A blacksmith named Fred La Rose was working at his forge near the railway construction site when he saw a fox staring at him from behind a rock. For some unknown reason Fred threw his hammer at the fox. He missed, but when he went to retrieve his hammer he found that it had chipped a large piece of the rock. The rock had a metallic shine that turned out to be one of the world's richest silver veins.

Over the years the rock around Cobalt gave up more than 420 million ounces of silver, worth more than $264,000,000. The legend of the "Cobalt Fox" is well known to those who live in this northern area. I enjoyed hearing it as well.

SATURDAY — FEBRUARY 24

NEW opinions are always suspected, and usually opposed without any other reason but because they are not already common.

—John Locke

SUNDAY — FEBRUARY 25

JESUS was walking by the Sea of Galilee when he saw Simon and his brother Andrew on the beach at work with a casting net, for they were fishermen. Jesus said to them, "Come with me and I will make you fishers of men." And at once they left their nets and followed him.

—Mark 1: 16-18

MONDAY — FEBRUARY 26

PATIENCE is the ability to put up with people you'd like to put down.

TUESDAY — FEBRUARY 27

THIS is a bit of trivia that I found interesting. In colonial days housewives had a rather strange way of keeping their furniture and floors clean without today's waxes and soaps. They spat on the floor and rubbed hard with stick brushes and reed brooms. This is where the expression "spit and polish" came from.

WEDNESDAY — FEBRUARY 28

Ash Wednesday

THEN He will answer them saying, "Truly I say to you, to the extent that you did not do it to one of the least of these, you did not do it to Me."

—Matthew 25: 45

March

THURSDAY — MARCH 1

ALTHOUGH it is not a well-known fact, this is an important date in American history. The Peace Corps was born on this date in 1961. Unlike other American help abroad, the Corps did not provide a flow of supplies to poorer nations. Instead, it was made up of people helping people—volunteers going abroad to share their know-how by working side by side with native farmers, doctors, and teachers.

This program of aid was the brainchild of John F. Kennedy, then President of the United States. Today, the work of the Peace Corps remains a significant monument to the slain President.

THE HERITAGE BOOK

SLAYER of winter, art thou here again?
O welcome, thou that bringst the summer
   nigh!
The bitter wind makes not thy victory vain.
Nor will we mock thee for thy faint blue sky.
Welcome, O March! Whose kindly days and
   dry
Make April ready for the throstle's song,
Thou first redresser of the winter's wrong!

Yea, welcome March! And though I die ere
   June,
Yet for the hope of life I give thee praise,
Striving to swell the burden of the tune
That even now I hear the brown birds raise,
Unmindful of the past or coming days;
Who sing "O joy! A new year is begun!
What happiness to look upon the sun!"
                              —*William Morris*

A person's education continues only as long
as his ignorance is exceeded by his curio-
sity.
                              —*Wanda Cunningham*

Sunday — March 4

Almighty God, your son fasted forty days in the wilderness, and was tempted but did not sin. Give us grace to discipline ourselves in submission to your spirit, that as you know our weakness, so may we know your power to save; through Jesus Christ our Lord, who is alive and reigns with you and the Holy Spirit, one God now and forever, Amen.

Monday — March 5

One of my favourite places to be at this time of year is in the shopping malls. No, I have not become a shopaholic. But now, when the weather is unsettled, I like to use the warm indoor malls as a place to walk. Marg drops me off at the entrance and then she leaves to do errands. I spend the next hour walking and window shopping, admiring the brightly coloured spring fashions.

This time enables me to exercise without battling the elements outdoors. I recommend it highly.

THE HERITAGE BOOK

I received surprising news in a letter today from my friend Peggy in England. Peggy has lived alone for years in a small home in the Cotswalds, a very lovely area in the English countryside about an hour's drive from London. In her letter she explains her intentions to turn her home into a "Bed and Breakfast" establishment.

"You know how beautiful it is here in the countryside, Edna. In our little town there are several small inns but they have become quite dear. I thought it would be nice if visitors had a place to stay that was more affordable, particularly for elderly people or young couples with small children. As well, it would supplement my small pension and give me a chance to have company and meet new friends. It has often been lonely since John's passing."

Peggy has redecorated the two upstairs bedrooms and added a bathroom exclusively for the guests. Knowing how Peggy keeps house, her guests will be certain to enjoy spotless rooms and wonderful, hearty breakfasts. I wish her well in this endeavour.

WEDNESDAY — MARCH 7

As a work of art, I know few things more pleasing to the eye, or more capable of affording scope and gratification to a taste for the beautiful, than a well situated, well cultivated farm.

—Edward Everett

THURSDAY — MARCH 8

This morning I was very surprised to see a robin in the backyard. I have always looked forward to seeing these harbingers of spring, but I am sure this poor little thing is simply premature in his arrival here in the north. Fortunately, Marg has put a fresh suet ball in the tree branches, so if he becomes desperate he will have something with which to fend off starvation.

Perhaps we will have an early spring after all.

FRIDAY — MARCH 9

The itching sensation that some people mistake for ambition is merely inflammation of the wishbone.

THE HERITAGE BOOK

RECENTLY it has become very popular to "collect." People are collecting everything from bottle caps to cameras to straw hats—including cookie cutters, metal doorstops, and keychains.

My good friend Jake Frampton has been collecting hockey cards for a number of years and he has amassed an enviable number of cards, both from recent years and years long past.

Jake has his collection displayed in his book-store and many of his customers have become avid "traders" of their own collections. I was astonished to learn that these collections are very valuable. People will often pay thousands of dollars for just one of the old cards.

Jake enjoys his collection immensely and that is certainly the best reason to "collect" anything.

GOD loved the world so much that he gave his only son, that everyone who has faith in Him may not die but have eternal life.

—*John 3: 16*

MONDAY — MARCH 12

ONE of the things I find very difficult as I get older is to like changes. I have certain clothing that gets worn often, not because it is stylish and good-looking, but because it is comfortable and old.

I prefer much of the "old-fashioned" music to today's songs sung by people with such strange names as Madonna or Purple Peter.

I like girls who wear their hair tied with a pretty ribbon. I really don't like hair that is bright green and standing on end.

This of course makes me feel old and many times I really work at giving new looks and ideas a chance.

One of the easier ways to feel youthful is to try a new recipe. This may sound foolish but it's really not so at all. I pride myself on being a good cook but it is very rare that I will make anything "new." My old, trusted, tried and true recipes are what I enjoy and feel good about serving. When I feel moved to "change" I will serve a meal that features items I have never tried before. Often I am surprised to find that I really enjoy these meals and that I have had fun preparing them.

Ah well, perhaps old dogs . . . .

THE HERITAGE BOOK

THAT man is a success who has lived well, laughed often and loved much; who has gained the respect of intelligent men and the love of children; who has filled his niche and accomplished his task; who leaves the world better than he found it, whether by an improved poppy, a perfect poem or a rescued soul; who never lacked appreciation of earth's beauty or failed to express it; who looked for the best in others and gave the best he had.

—Robert Louis Stevenson

GIVER of the perfect gift,
Only hope of human race,
Hear the prayer our hearts uplift
Gathered at thy throne of grace.

Oh may these our Lenten days
Blessed by thee, with thee be passed
That with purer, nobler praise
We may keep thy feast at last.

—John Ellerton

THURSDAY — MARCH 15

IF faith can move mountains imagine what hard work can do.

FRIDAY — MARCH 16

I hope you enjoy Nora Hopper's poem "March" as much as I have.

Blossom on the plum
Wild wind and merry;
Leaves upon the cherry,
And one swallow come.

Red windy dawn,
Swift rain and sunny;
Wild bees seeking honey,
Crocus on the lawn;
Blossom on the plum.

Grass begins to grow,
Dandelions come;
Snowdrops haste to go
After last month's snow;
Rough winds beat and blow,
Blossoms on the plum.

SATURDAY — MARCH 17

THE man who has not anything to boast of but his illustrious ancestors is like a potato —the only good belonging to him is underground.

—Mark Twain

SUNDAY — MARCH 18

WE rejoice in our suffering knowing that suffering produces endurance, and endurance produces character, and character produces hope, and hope does not disappoint us because God's love has been poured into our hearts through the Holy Spirit, which has been given to us.

—Romans 5: 3-5

MONDAY — MARCH 19

BE not afraid of life. Believe that life is worth living and your belief will help create the fact.

—William James

THE HERITAGE BOOK

ONE of the most important volunteer groups in our area is the "M.O.W." or Meals On Wheels. The drivers for this organization deliver hot meals once a day to individuals who are chronically ill, disabled, convalescing, or just too old to shop for groceries. The meals, which are subsidized by several government agencies, are usually made in local nursing homes or hospitals.

Because it is a "low-key" group there are times when drivers become scarce. When this happened recently in our area the organization received help from an unexpected source.

Members of the students' council at the high school voted to make Meals on Wheels a school project. Many of the needy people in our area can now look forward to receiving their meals and a friendly visit from young men and women who care enough about these people to give tangible help.

Wednesday — March 21

WRINKLES are just God's etchings.

THURSDAY — MARCH 22

SPRING! Ah, the sound of the word makes the heart dance and sing. Spring!

FRIDAY — MARCH 23

BRUCE came home from work today with a delightful surprise for Marg and me. When he was in the city today he stopped at the market and got us each a magnificent basket of tulips and daffodils.

Many of the plants are now in bloom but there are more still unopened. When we have enjoyed the flowers indoors we can then transplant the bulbs to the garden to bloom again next spring.

I feel extremely fortunate to have such a thoughtful son-in-law.

SATURDAY — MARCH 24

MAY I carry, if I will,
All your burdens up the hill?
And she answered with a laugh,
No, but you may carry half.

THE HERITAGE BOOK

THERE is a green hill far away
Outside a city wall,
Where the dear Lord was crucified
Who died to save us all.

There was no other good enough
To pay the price of sin.
He only could unlock the gate
Of heaven, and let us in.
—*Cecil Frances Alexander*

MONDAY — MARCH 26

ON this day back in 1885 George Eastman created a communications miracle when he manufactured the first commercial motion-picture film.

It was a simple idea that he developed, but it played a dramatic role in the communications revolution. Great dramas and news-breaking events could be captured on film and shown countrywide.

Were he alive today I'm sure Mr. Eastman would be impressed with the film and cameras that have evolved from his simple idea of so long ago.

THE HERITAGE BOOK

M Y daughter Mary and her husband John stopped in for dinner this evening. John is a minister and their life closely parallels the life that George and I spent together. I find it so nostalgic listening to their stories of parish life. There are always many amusing anecdotes for John to relate and tonight was no exception.

"This past weekend I was approached by one of the elderly widows of the parish who said she needed to speak with me in private. We retired to my office and she told me that she had a confession to make. 'This has bothered me all winter, John, so I wanted to get it off my chest. Do you remember last fall when you returned from your hunting trip and gave me two ducks? Later, when you asked if I enjoyed them I said yes. Well, John, I lied to you because I didn't have the heart to tell you that I had no idea how to pluck them or clean them or cook them so I just took them out to my backyard and buried them'.

"Edna, I still haven't stopped laughing."

WEDNESDAY — MARCH 28

NOSTALGIA is longing for a place you wouldn't move back to.

THURSDAY — MARCH 29

THERE'S so much spectating going on that a lot of us never get around to living. Life is always walking up to us and saying, "Come on in, the living's fine." And what do we do? Back off and take its picture.

—Russell Babes

FRIDAY — MARCH 30

IF you don't enjoy what you have, how could you be happier with more?

SATURDAY — MARCH 31

IF you treat everybody courteously, it will surprise you how courteous they all become.

April

Sunday — April 1

ALMIGHTY God, your Son came into the world to free us from sin and death. Grant that we may always live in the perfect freedom of His service, through Jesus Christ our Lord, who is alive and reigns with you and the Holy Spirit, one God, now and forever. Amen.

Monday — April 2

GUARD within yourself that treasure, kindness. Know how to give without hesitation, how to lose without regret, how to acquire without meanness. Know how to replace in your heart, by the happiness of those you love, the happiness that may be wanting to yourself.

—*George Sand*

THE HERITAGE BOOK

DOCTORS who specialize in gerontology, the study of aging, suggest that there are four basic requirements for successful aging. These are: a variety of meaningful activities; good health habits (exercise and proper eating); sound financial planning; and perhaps most importantly, an optimistic outlook.

Studies show that the happiest older people seem to have achieved a balance of different activities—group, solitary, active, passive, etc. While family is very important in these activities, peer association and communication are also crucial.

Exercise and good eating habits are essential as we grow older. It is important therefore to develop these early, since it is more difficult to break bad habits or establish good ones later in life.

Professional advice in financial decisions will often help us to maximize our income. Government help also keeps us comfortable.

Being optimistic can add years to our lives.

With all of these we can look forward to enjoying long and happy lives.

Wednesday — April 4

In the tiny village of St. Aniset, Québec, Ernest Léger, a storekeeper, showed great faith in his two sons. Instead of doling out their allowance he left the store's cash box open, allowing the boys to help themselves to their designated sums.

Some villagers felt this was an unfair temptation to the boys, and told Ernest so. M. Léger saw it in a different light, as a daily testament of his faith and trust.

It would seem his faith was justified. The younger son, Jules, became a Governor General of Canada. The older, Paul-Emile, became a Cardinal in the Catholic Church.

Thursday — April 5

Laughter is God's gift to mankind and mankind is the proof that God has a sense of humour.

Friday — April 6

A wedding is an event, but marriage is an achievement.

THE HERITAGE BOOK

<u>Saturday — April 7</u>

Sang the sunrise on an April morn—
"Earth, be glad! An April day is born.

Winter's done, and April's in the skies,
Earth, look up with laughter in your eyes.

Putting off her dumb dismay of snow,
Earth bade all her unseen children grow.

Then the sound of growing in the air
Rose to God a liturgy of prayer;

And the thronged succession of the days
Uttered up to God a psalm of praise.

Laughed the running sap in every vein,
Laughed the running flurries of warm rain,

Laughed the life in every wandering root,
Laughed the tingling cells of bud and shoot.

God is all the concord of their mirth
Heard the adoration-song of Earth.

                              —*Charles G.D. Roberts*

THE HERITAGE BOOK

Palm Sunday

THE disciples went and did as Jesus had directed, and brought the donkey and her foal; they laid their cloaks on them and Jesus mounted. Crowds of people carpeted the roads with their cloaks, and some cut branches from the trees to spread in his path. Then the crowd that went ahead and the other that came behind raised the shout "Hosanna to the Son of David! Blessings on him who comes in the name of the Lord. Hosanna in the heavens."

—Matthew 21: 6-9

THE HERITAGE BOOK

MONDAY — APRIL 9

SILENCES make the real conversations between friends. Not the saying but the never
needing to say is what counts.

TUESDAY — APRIL 10

THERE are only two lasting bequests we can
hope to give our children. One of these is
roots; the other, wings.

WEDNESDAY — APRIL 11

IF you talk about your troubles,
And you tell 'em o'er and o'er,
Sure, the world will think you like 'em,
And proceed to give you more!

—John Scott

THURSDAY — APRIL 12

MY friend Mary McConnell has a very large family. She and her husband are raising ten children, something almost unheard of in this day and age.

Travelling with a family of this size could be difficult at best. However, Mary has come up with an excellent idea to keep the children entertained and happy on long trips.

"Before we set off we collect all of our loose photos and I buy several photo albums. We pass the hours in the car very happily remembering the times pictured in our photos. We then arrange the photos into the albums and by the time we have finished we have usually arrived at our destination."

FRIDAY — APRIL 13

Good Friday

THEY took Jesus, and he went out, carrying his own cross to the place called the place of a skull, which is called in Hebrew, Golgotha. There they crucified him, and with him two others, one on either side and Jesus in between them. Pilate also wrote a title and put it on the cross; it read "Jesus of Nazareth, the King of the Jews."

—John 19: 17-19

SATURDAY — APRIL 14

HAVE you noticed that people who try to give you advice never seem quite as intelligent as those who ask for yours?

SUNDAY — APRIL 15

Easter Sunday

MARY Magdalene went and said to his disciples "I have seen the Lord."

—John 20: 18

THE HERITAGE BOOK

THERE is no man living who is not capable of doing more than he thinks he can do.
—*Henry Ford*

ONE of the most popular programs ever to air on North American television was "Bonanza." The role of Ben Cartwright, the grey-haired patriarch of the Ponderosa, was played by Lorne Greene. Such was the skill of this actor that, in the minds of millions of viewers, Ben Cartwright and Lorne Greene were one.

Lorne Green was born in Ottawa in 1915. While attending Queen's University in Kingston he was awarded a scholarship to the Neighbourhood Playhouse School of the Theatre in New York, where he studied acting. During the war years he was the chief newscaster for the CBC. Lorne Greene's big break came when he was cast in the long-running "Bonanza." He remained active in television until his death in 1987.

Lorne Greene was a marvellous actor and a credit to Canada.

WEDNESDAY — APRIL 18

As I walked through the neighbourhood to-day I was happy to see the crocus shoots coming up in many of the gardens.

This is such a hopeful time of year. No matter how long a winter it has been the promise of renewed life on the trees in our gardens seems to give everyone a lift.

I remember well the first spring after George's passing. It had been a long and hard winter. My grief was intense and at times overwhelming. I could hardly believe that life would go on as before—and then spring came. All around me the signs were obvious. The leaves were budding, the birds had returned and were singing, and at last I could see the renewal of God's promise of an everlasting world. The sun, with its promise of warmer days, cheered me as little else had all winter.

As I walked on that spring day I looked around and realized that life does go on—and I could go on too.

THURSDAY — APRIL 19

I want a warm and faithful friend,
To cheer the adverse hour;
Who ne'er to flatter will descend,
Nor bend the knee to power.
A friend to chide me when I'm wrong,
My inmost soul to see;
And that my friendship proves as strong
To him as his to me.

—John Quincy Adams

FRIDAY — APRIL 20

Good temper, like a sunny day, sheds a brightness over everything; it is the sweetener of toil and the soother of disquietude.

SATURDAY — APRIL 21

Perhaps the secret of life is to run out of years before we run out of dreams.

THE HERITAGE BOOK

JESUS said 'Because you have seen me you have found faith, Thomas. Happy are those who never saw me and yet have found faith'.

—*John 20: 29*

ONE of the most difficult decisions facing young families today is whether both parents will work. In many cases it is not a matter of choice—both mother and father work because they need two incomes. However in other instances it is an option.

I guess I am old-fashioned but I feel very strongly that if at all possible one of the two parents should be at home with young children. The first five years of a child's life are so very important. I would not have missed my girls' babyhood for anything. Their first smiles, their first tentative steps—these were moments of great joy for me.

If I could offer advice to young parents it would be, "Stay home—it's worth the financial sacrifice."

TUESDAY — APRIL 24

A truthful recognition of our own ignorance is a foot on the doorstep to the temple of wisdom.

—Ruth Brown

WEDNESDAY — APRIL 25

THE "Prayer for Generosity," given to us by St. Ignatius Loyola, has long been a favourite of mine.

Teach us, good Lord, to serve Thee as Thou
    deservest:
To give and not to count the cost;
To fight and not to heed the wounds;
To toil and not to seek for rest;
To labour and not ask for any reward
Save that of knowing that we do Thy will.

THURSDAY — APRIL 26

A real friend is one who walks in when the rest of the world walks out.

—Walter Winchell

THE HERITAGE BOOK

MANY of us tend to take the people who work as firefighters very much for granted. This poem reminds us how much is on the line each time they are called upon to fight to save one of us.

When I am called to duty, God,
Wherever flames may rage,
Give me strength to save some life
Whatever be its age;
Help me to embrace a little child,
Before it is too late
Or save an older person from
The horror of that fate;
Enable me to be alert
And hear the weakest shout,
And quickly and efficiently
To put the fire out.
I want to fill my calling and
To give the best in me,
To guard my every neighbour and
Protect his property;
And if, according to Your will,
I have to leave my life,
Please bless with your protecting hand
My children and my wife.

SATURDAY — APRIL 28

A major form of charity is giving someone the benefit of the doubt.

SUNDAY — APRIL 29

LET the people praise you O God. Let all the people praise you. We glory in your cross, O Lord, and praise and glorify your holy resurrection—for by virtue of your cross, joy has come to the whole world; let the people praise you, O God.

—Book of Alternative Services

MONDAY — APRIL 30

NO one is a failure in this world who lightens a burden for someone else.

May

It is not raining rain for me,
It's raining daffodils;
In every dimpled drop I see
Wild flowers on the hills.

The clouds of gray engulf the day
And overwhelm the town;
It is not raining rain to me,
It's raining roses down.

It is not raining rain to me,
But fields of clover bloom,
There any buccaneering bee
Can find a bed and room.

A health unto the happy,
A fig for him who frets!
It is not raining rain to me,
It's raining violets.

—*Robert Loveman*

THE HERITAGE BOOK

WHENEVER Marg or Bruce drive me to the Senior Citizens' Centre in early spring I enjoy a very special treat. The road leading to the Centre is adjacent to an old estate in which the wild spring flowers grow in profusion.

The trilliums, both white and red, crowd around the trunks of tall maple and beechnut trees. We will often pull over to the edge of the road to admire these beautiful blooms as they glow in the filtered sunlight.

It brings back memories of wooded hikes I took as a child with my brother and sister. The first time we saw trilliums we were unaware that it was forbidden to pick these majestic blooms. We came home with our small hands filled with what we thought was a wonderful treat for Mother. She explained patiently to us that these flowers were to be looked at only, never picked.

These flowers bring wonderful memories and a wealth of beauty to the eye.

THURSDAY — MAY 3

THE fact that something is beyond your vision doesn't mean it isn't there.

THE HERITAGE BOOK

MY friend Jake Frampton had an amusing story to tell me today. He and his friend John were driving together when John braked rather suddenly to avoid hitting a mother duck followed by several baby ducks crossing the road.

A woman in the car behind John's rolled down her window and called out impatiently, "Why don't you honk your horn?"

John's reply silenced her effectively. "I think, madam, that the ducks are already walking as fast as they can."

SATURDAY — MAY 5

TRY to do unto others as you would have them do to you, and do not be discouraged if they fail sometimes. It is much better that they should fail than that you should.

—Charles Dickens

SUNDAY — MAY 6

LET everything that has breath praise the Lord. Praise the Lord!

—Psalm 150: 6

MONDAY — MAY 7

However mean your life is, meet it and live it; do not shun it and call it hard names. It is not so bad as you are. It looks poorest when you are richest. The fault finder will find fault even in paradise.

—Henry David Thoreau

TUESDAY — MAY 8

There is an interesting account from the Second World War that I enjoyed very much.

As happened in many European countries, the Jewish people in Denmark were deported from their homes and country.

During this time the Danes took personal care of the houses of all deported Jews. They kept them spotlessly clean and their gardens well tended. When the survivors returned they found their homes in beautiful condition and their rooms filled with flowers from their gardens.

What a wonderful welcome home it must have been for them. Even in terrible times there can be some small measure of help and hope.

THE HERITAGE BOOK

WEDNESDAY — MAY 9

My son-in-law Bruce knows how much I love stories about the great Canadian writer Stephen Leacock. Bruce read this story in a Reader's Digest of several years ago.

A reporter was sent to Leacock's Toronto hotel room to interview the writer. Leacock asked the reporter if she would mind waiting just a few minutes while he addressed the letters he had just written.

When he was finished he walked to the window and tossed the letters out to the sidewalk below.

The startled journalist asked why he had thrown his letters away when he had taken the trouble to address and stamp them.

Leacock just smiled and replied, "If you saw a stamped letter on the street wouldn't you pick it up and put it in a mailbox?"

THURSDAY — MAY 10

America is great not because of what government did for the people but because of what government permitted a free people to do for themselves.

—American Congressman Collins

Friday — May 11

I enjoyed Henry Timrod's poem "Spring" this morning. I hope you will enjoy it as well.

Spring, with that nameless pathos in the air
Which dwells with all things fair,
Spring, with her golden suns and silver rain,
Is with us once again.

Out in the woods the jasmine burns
Its fragrant lamps, and turns
Into a royal court with green festoons
The banks of dark lagoons.

In the deep heart of every forest tree
The blood is all aglee,
And there's a look about the leafless bowers
As if they dreamed of flowers.

Yet still on every side we trace the hand
Of Winter in the land,
Save where the maple reddens on the lawn,
Flushed by the season's dawn;

Or where, like those strange semblances we
find
That age to childhood blind,
The elm puts on, as if in Nature's scorn,
The brown of autumn corn.

SATURDAY — MAY 12

THE superior man is distressed by the limitations of his ability; he is not distressed by the fact that men do not recognize the ability he has.

—Confucius

SUNDAY — MAY 13

Mother's Day

THE courage that my mother had
Went with her, and is with her still.
Rock from New England quarried;
Now Granite in a granite hill.

The golden broach my mother wore
She left behind for me to wear;
I have no thing I treasure more:
Yet it is something I could spare.

Oh if instead she'd left to me
The things she took into the grave!
That courage like a rock, which she
Has no more need of, and I have.

—Edna St. Vincent Millay

THE HERITAGE BOOK

A good friend of mine is an insurance agent with a large Canadian company. Recently his company distributed a letter that listed amusing accident descriptions submitted by policy holders with his firm. I found several of them to be very entertaining, as I hope you will.

"The other car collided with mine without giving warning of its intention."

"I thought my window was down, but found it was up when I put my hand through it."

"A pedestrian hit me and went under my car."

"The pedestrian had no idea which direction to go, so I ran him over."

"Coming home, I drove into the wrong house and collided with a tree I don't have."

"To avoid hitting the bumper of the car in front, I struck the pedestrian."

THE HERITAGE BOOK

THIS is a time of year when parents start thinking of plans for their children's summer vacation. In many families these plans include summer camp. There are many wonderful camps available for children; camps with extraordinary facilities for swimming, sailing, water-skiing, and all of the other activities that youngsters enjoy on warm summer days.

I have heard recently of a new and interesting camp for grandparents and their grandchildren. It is set in a traditional camp setting, in the woods by a lake. There are sleeping cabins and a large mess hall for meals. The difference is that the children stay together with a counsellor in cabins while grandparents stay in rooms much like a small motel.

Children and their grandparents eat together and participate in many of the camp activities, such as sailing or campfire weiner roasts. It can be a precious time for all, without the grandparents having the responsibility of making meals or having to keep up the pace of the youngsters.

What a wonderful and innovative idea.

WEDNESDAY — MAY 16

EVERY man prays in his own language, but there is no language that God does not understand.

—*Duke Ellington*

THURSDAY — MAY 17

AN old-fashioned woman is a gal who tries to make one husband last a lifetime.

FRIDAY — MAY 18

NORMAN Rockwell was one of my favourite artists. I think he summed up very well why his work has remained popular for generations when he said, "People somehow get out of your work just about what you put into it and if you are interested in the characters you draw and understand and love them why, the person who sees your picture is bound to feel the same way."

THE HERITAGE BOOK

I have developed a great fondness for muffins and today I would like to share with you one of my favourite recipes—for apricot bran muffins.

1 1/4 cups all-purpose flour
1 cup natural bran
1/3 cup brown sugar
1 tbsp. baking powder
3/4 tsp. cinnamon
1 egg, 1 ripe banana mashed, 1/3 cup honey, 1/3 cup melted butter, 3/4 cup milk, 2/3 cup chopped dried apricots.

Stir together flour, bran, brown sugar, baking powder, and cinnamon. In a separate bowl, beat the egg lightly. Stir in mashed banana, honey, butter, and milk. Stir flour mixture into the milk mixture just until blended. Mix in the apricots.

Spoon the batter into buttered muffin pans. Bake in a preheated 400° oven for 20-25 minutes.

This recipe makes 1 dozen muffins.

THE HERITAGE BOOK

<u>Sunday — May 20</u>

Fairest Lord Jesus,
  Ruler of all nature,
O thou of God and man the son
Thee will I cherish, thee will I honour
Thou my soul's glory, joy and crown.
                    —*From 17th century Germany*

<u>Monday — May 21</u>

This is the first of the season's long weekends, and like the past several years we
spent it in Muskoka, helping my good friend
Eleanor open her cottage.

Although it was not a particularly warm
weekend several of the neighbouring children
were happily pushing one another off the dock
into the chilly water.

Later in the afternoon we were entertained
by a group of windsurfers sailing by, their
multicoloured sails bright in the sunlight.

Ah, youth . . . .

Tuesday — May 22

WHEN I consider what some books have done for the world, and what they are doing, how they keep up our hope, awaken new courage and faith, soothe pain, give an ideal life to those whose hours are cold and hard, bind together distant ages and foreign lands, create new worlds of beauty, bring down truth from heaven; I give eternal blessing for this gift and thank God for books.

—*James Freeman Clarke*

Wednesday — May 23

WE have been watching the bird feeder from our kitchen window. The joy brought by each new group of birds greatly repays us for our efforts to feed them a little. The purple finches are new in our neighbourhood this spring; they are accompanied by endless chickadees. The birds remind us of the words of the sixteenth-century writer Edmund Spencer.

"The merry cuckoo messenger of Spring, his triumphant shrill hath thrice already sounded."

Thursday — May 24

Q UEEN Victoria, the late British monarch, was born on this date in 1819. A very young woman when she became queen, she was the longest reigning monarch in British history.

She married her cousin Prince Albert in 1840, and their marriage produced nine children. Albert played a very active part in the management of all her affairs, both public and private. Following his death in 1861 Victoria went into deep mourning for the remainder of her life.

The strength of Queen Victoria lay in her good common sense and directness of character. She expressed those qualities of the British nation that, at the time, made it preeminent in the world.

Friday — May 25

L IFE may be like a game of cards; we cannot help the hand that is dealt us but we can help the way we play it.

—*Bishop Fulton Sheen*

SATURDAY — MAY 26

For each and every joyful thing,
For twilight swallows on the wing,
For all that nest and all that sing,—

For fountains cool that laugh and leap,
For rivers running to the deep,
For happy, care-forgetting sleep,—

For stars that pierce the sombre dark,
For morn, awaking with the lark,
For life new stirring 'neath the bark,—

For sunshine and the blessed rain,
For budding grove and blossomy lane,
For the sweet silence of the plain,—

For bounty springing from the sod,
For every step by beauty trod,—
For each dear gift of joy, thank God!
—*Florence Earle Coates*

SUNDAY — MAY 27

This is the day which the Lord hath made;
we will rejoice and be glad in it.
—*Psalm 118: 24*

MONDAY — MAY 28

MY good friends Will and Muriel stopped by for tea this afternoon and it wasn't long before Will was out in the garden, "just puttering," as he put it.

Will enjoys gardening—his flower beds are the envy of his neighbours—and he takes great pleasure in giving Marg, Bruce, and me all kinds of help with our gardens. His ideas are invariably excellent and, thanks to Will, our flowers are looking more and more lovely every year.

What I think is wonderful is the great pleasure Will gets from working in the garden. His eyes light up and his speech becomes animated as he talks about different plants or flowers. His obvious enjoyment gives those around him a sense of happiness as well.

TUESDAY — MAY 29

NEVER look down to test the ground before taking your next step: only he who keeps his eyes fixed on the far horizon will find the right road.

—*Dag Hammarskjöld*

WEDNESDAY — MAY 30

LILA Acheson Wallace, the Canadian-born co-founder of Reader's Digest, passed away in 1984 at the age of ninety-four.

Lila and her husband DeWitt compiled a fortune together, and together they gave much of it away.

She often said that she had memorized her will. It read "I, Lila Acheson Wallace, being of sound mind and body . . . spent it."

THURSDAY — MAY 31

GREAT people are ordinary people with extraordinary amounts of determination.

June

Love is like magic
And it always will be,
For love still remains
Life's sweet mystery!

Love can transform
The most commonplace
Into beauty and splendour
And sweetness and grace!

Love is unselfish,
Understanding and kind,
For it sees with its heart
And not with its mind!

Love can't be bought,
It is priceless and free,
Love like pure magic
Is a sweet mystery!

—*Helen Steiner Rice*

SATURDAY — JUNE 2

MONEY will buy a bed but not sleep; books but not brains; food but not appetite; finery but not beauty; a house but not a home; medicine but not health; luxury but not culture; amusements but not happiness; religion but not salvation; a passport to everywhere but heaven.

SUNDAY — JUNE 3

FOR many of us, today is truly the birthday of the Church. It was through the gift of God's holy spirit that the disciples were strengthened and enabled to fulfill our Lord's command—"Go forth and make all nations my disciple."

"While the day of Pentecost was running its course, they were all together in one place when suddenly there came from the sky a noise like that of a strong striving wind, which filled the whole house where they were sitting. And there appeared to them tongues like flames of fire, dispersed among them and resting on each one. And they were filled with the Holy Spirit."

—Acts 2: 1-4

Monday — June 4

HOLDING on to anger is like grasping a hot coal with the intent of throwing it at someone else—you are the one who gets burned.

—Buddha

Tuesday — June 5

TUESDAY is my usual day to visit our local library and today was no exception. After Marg dropped me off this morning I walked up the steps, prepared to pass my usual quiet hour selecting my reading for the week. However, today's visit was a little different.

There was a class of grade one students with their teacher listening intently to the librarian as she explained how each of them could borrow books with their "very own card."

It was a treat to see the enthusiasm these youngsters showed in choosing their books. Several of them asked my help in selecting appropriate books, and I was more than happy to oblige.

It made my day a happier one to know that these children were getting a good start in the exciting world of reading.

THE HERITAGE BOOK

ONE of the most tragic things I know about human nature is that all of us tend to put off living. We dream of some magical rose garden over the horizon—instead of enjoying the roses that are blooming outside our window today.

—*Dale Carnegie*

AROUND this time of year the universities and colleges hold their graduation exercises.

Marg and Bruce attended the graduation of the son of close friends. Bruce came in chuckling loudly. The guest speaker had tickled everyone's fancy with his opening remarks.

"I have never understood the logic of commencement exercises. Here are five hundred people in caps with funny-looking tassels, sitting on hard wooden chairs and wearing heavy black gowns in the blazing afternoon sun—being told how smart they are."

<u>Friday — June 8</u>

If you ever wonder what the world is coming to, remember, so did your grandfather.

<u>Saturday — June 9</u>

One of the more pleasant aspects of a birthday at my age is that it provides a nice opportunity for a family get-together.

Today the family held a lovely party for me at the country home of my grandson Fred and his wife June. It was a "pot luck" luncheon and the food was simply delicious. Ham, turkey, scalloped potatoes, endless salads, and hot biscuits loaded the tables to the full.

The children had a grand time playing hide-and-seek in the woods. This gave the adults some quiet time for conversation, and a chance to visit with those whom they haven't seen in some time.

A surprise guest was my dear friend Emily, who travelled from Philadelphia to wish me a happy birthday.

All in all it was well worth adding yet another year to my total.

SUNDAY — JUNE 10

O Father, my hope.
O Son, my refuge.
O Holy Spirit, my protection
Holy Trinity, glory to Thee.
—Comptine-St. Joannikios
- Eastern Orthodox

MONDAY — JUNE 11

To be able to lead others, a man must be willing to go forward alone.
—Abraham Kaplan

TUESDAY — JUNE 12

IF a man could mount to heaven and survey the mighty universe, his admiration of its beauties would be much diminished unless he had someone to share in his pleasure.

WEDNESDAY — JUNE 13

More than 120 years ago a thirty-five-year-old man opened a little store on the southwest corner of Yonge and Queen Streets in Toronto. This new store employed a startlingly new concept: goods would have a set, marked price—no bartering. The goods would be sold for cash only, and with the promise, "Satisfactory or money refunded."

Experienced merchants predicted disaster but the business defied these prophesies and soon outgrew its original location. It moved to 190 Yonge Street, just north of Queen. By the early 1890s the business had become "Canada's Greatest Store" and Timothy Eaton had laid down the principles on which the Eatons store still stands: "Goods Satisfactory or Money Refunded. No One Importuned to Buy ... One Price Only."

A great factor in Timothy Eaton's success was his ability to choose his men wisely. He seemed always to choose the right man for the job and each man was given unlimited opportunity to make good.

The fact that Eatons remains today one of Canada's greatest stores is a tribute to its founder, Timothy Eaton.

THURSDAY — JUNE 14

A sense of humour is a shock absorber on the road of life.

FRIDAY — JUNE 15

WE may elevate ourselves but we should never reach so high that we would ever forget those who helped us get there.

SATURDAY — JUNE 16

THE rung of a ladder was never meant to rest upon, but only to hold a man's foot long enough to enable him to put the other somewhat higher.

—Thomas Henry Huxley

THE HERITAGE BOOK

<u>SUNDAY — JUNE 17</u>

THE word of the Lord holds true, and all his work endures. The Lord loves righteousness and justice, his love unfailing fills the earth. Happy the people chosen by the Lord.

—*Psalm 33: 4-5, 12*

<u>MONDAY — JUNE 18</u>

THIS can be a time of despair for teachers. If a student fails to do well by the end of the school year it is often perceived by the teacher as his or her own failure.

British pediatrician Ronald Illingworth compiled this list of school failures.

Poor spellers: Yeats, Shaw
Poor mathematicians: Franklin, Picasso, Adler, Jung
Expelled from school: Einstein, Poe, Shelley, Röntgen, Whistler
Bottom of the class: Edison
Dreamer: Gauguin
"Dull and Inept": Watt
Mentally Slow: Einstein

THE HERITAGE BOOK

KINDNESS is so vital in a world that would be happy. Many writers have offered their thoughts on kindness. Here are but a few.

Kind words are the music of the world. They have a power which seems to be beyond natural causes, as though they were some angel's song which had lost its way and come to earth.
—*Frederick William Faber*

Kindness is a language which the deaf man can hear and the blind man read.
—*Mark Twain*

A kind heart is a fountain of gladness making everything in its vicinity freshen into smiles.
—*Washington Irving*

Kindness in woman, not their beauteous looks, shall win my love.
—*"The Taming of the Shrew,"*
William Shakespeare

Great persons are able to do great kindnesses.
—*Miguel de Cervantes*

WEDNESDAY — JUNE 20

My son-in-law Bruce is an avid reader of interesting but little-known facts. He imparted this gem to Marg and me at dinner this evening.

Worshippers in the Great Mosque of Sivas, Turkey, kneel on carpets worth about fourteen million dollars. When the carpets in Turkish mosques wear out, new ones are laid on top of the old ones. The strata of carpets in the Sivas mosque date back to the eleventh century.

THURSDAY — JUNE 21

Fear of expressing ourselves makes prisoners of our thoughts.

—*Bern Williams*

FRIDAY — JUNE 22

Believe the best rather than the worse. People have a way of living up—or down—to your opinion of them.

THE HERITAGE BOOK

I had a telephone visit with my sister Sarah today. We correspond very regularly by letter but I really enjoy our less frequent phone calls. Nothing can take the place of hearing the voice of a loved one.

Sarah was telling me of her daily walks by the sea. "You know, Edna, there is nothing I enjoy more than a lovely long walk beside the ocean. I listen to the waves roll on the sand and smell the salty air. I sleep so well after a long afternoon walk; it clears my mind and relaxes me fully."

I was very interested to hear Sarah's comments on the relaxing effect of the ocean. I read recently that a study completed at the University of Warwick in England showed that the smells of the beach can soothe people suffering from severe forms of chronic anxiety. The researchers found that anxious patients became much less fearful after they smelled a "beach perfume" containing essence of seaweed and salt water.

It is an interesting concept and one with which Sarah would readily concur.

THE HERITAGE BOOK

SUNDAY — JUNE 24

The Festival of St. John the Baptist

O Jordan's bank, the Baptist cry
   announces that the Lord is nigh,
Awake and harken, for he brings
   glad tidings of the King of kings.

Then cleansed be every breast from sin
   make straight the way for God within,
Prepare we in our heart a home
   where such a mighty guest may come.
—Charles Colton, The Hymn Book

MONDAY — JUNE 25

TAKE time to be kind,
   Help those who have not;
Leave worries behind,
Give life your best shot!

TUESDAY — JUNE 26

LEARN the sweet magic of a cheerful face—
not always smiling, but at least serene.
—Oliver Wendell Holmes

WEDNESDAY — JUNE 27

FAILURES are more commonly caused by having made no choice than by wrong decisions.

—L. Carte

THURSDAY — JUNE 28

I have learned silence from the talkative, toleration from the intolerant, and kindness from the unkind; yet strange, I am ungrateful to those teachers.

—Kahlil Gibran

FRIDAY — JUNE 29

THIS little story is, perhaps, an indication of our times.

The boss called in his young manager to find out why he stayed late at the office day after day.

"Well, you see, sir," he said, red-faced, "my wife works too, and if I get home before she does, I have to make dinner."

THE HERITAGE BOOK

If I Should Stumble

IF I should stumble—as I have and will,
Oh, let me stumble going up the hill;
Let the stumbling be because my eyes
Are fixed upon some star high in the skies.

If I should fall—and I will have my share.
Let me fall going up the stair;
And let me not blame others for the pain,
But quietly arise and try again.

If I should stumble, let it be I seek
A precious foothold toward a mountain peak;
Or that I feel the challenge of the pace
Set by fleeter runners in life's race.

If I should stumble on my little mile,
Help me to make that stumbling worthwhile,
To recognize the blocks that fouled my way
And thus climb better on the coming day.

—Helen Lowrie Marshall

July

Canada Day

O Lord our God who dost will for all nations such good things as pass man's understanding, shape the desires and deeds of thy people in accordance with thy purpose for the world; that seeking first thy Kingdom and righteousness, we may be citizens of this realm and set forth the true welfare of mankind, through thy son, our Lord, Jesus Christ. Amen.

THE HERITAGE BOOK

Monday — July 2

OUR eyes are where they are for seeing opportunities ahead—not for looking behind at all of our mistakes.

Tuesday — July 3

DON'T be annoyed when your children ask impossible questions; be proud that they think you know the answers.

Wednesday — July 4

THIS is a special day for our American friends. The Fourth of July celebrates their independence and allows for the exuberant show of patriotism that is uniquely American.
Happy Birthday, America!

THE HERITAGE BOOK

Thursday — July 5

My friend Lila and I spent a most enjoyable day in the city of Welland, Ontario. We went on a "Seniors Bus Tour" to the Niagara Peninsula and to the town the canal built.

One of the most interesting parts of our day was spent at the Welland Historical Museum. This museum occupies a schoolhouse dating from 1914. Exhibits outline the history of Welland since the earliest days.

I learned that the region surrounding Welland was originally inhabited by the Neutral Indians, and that the United Empire Loyalists were the first Europeans to settle and farm. They were followed by Europeans seeking inexpensive farm lands, then by Irishmen coming to work on the construction of the canal.

Models in the museum indicate how the original canal, made of white pine, was replaced in 1845 by a more massive stone structure. In the years that followed the canal underwent two more modernizations, until in 1973 the present four-siphon culvert was installed.

Displays are plentiful and it is a most enjoyable place to spend a summer's day.

FRIDAY — JULY 6

ONE of the things I most enjoy in summer is our casual style of eating. My son-in-law, Bruce, is a whiz at the barbeque and we regularly have some barbequed chicken or fish with a fresh salad and homemade rolls. It is an easily made but delicious meal.

This evening was no exception. A good friend at Bruce's office sent home some lake trout he had caught on a fishing trip. Bruce did an extraordinary job cooking them, and combined with Marg's spinach and orange salad and my buttermilk biscuits it was a meal "fit for kings." The fact that we shared the dinner with friends outdoors on the patio made it twice as nice.

I find dinners eaten outside in the warmth of the summer's evening to be such a pleasant relief after the long winter.

SATURDAY — JULY 7

LAUGHTER is the hand of God on the shoulder of our troubled world.

THE HERITAGE BOOK

SUNDAY — JULY 8

Bᵧ their fruits you will recognize them . . . every good tree bears good fruit.

—*Matthew 7: 16-17*

MONDAY — JULY 9

Tᴏᴅᴀʏ is the fifth birthday of my great grandchildren, the twins Jenny and Justin.

It hardly seems possible that five years have passed since they were so tiny that they had to stay in the hospital until they grew bigger and stronger.

At their birthday party, celebrated yesterday, Justin was one of the biggest boys in his group of friends. (He was also one of the most energetic.) Jenny, while not as tall as Justin, is a very good size for her age.

Jenny and Justin have many friends but, as is often the case with twins, they are each other's best friend.

These little lines express it well:

To be a child, just one, is fun
When you are only one of one
But better still—I know it's true
To be a child when you are one of two.

THE HERITAGE BOOK

Tuesday — July 10

THE most certain way to succeed is always to try just one more time.

—*Thomas Edison*

Wednesday — July 11

AGE is opportunity no less than youth itself,
although in another dress.
And as the evening twilight fades away
The sky is filled with stars invisible by day.

—*Longfellow*

Thursday — July 12

LOVE is a fabric that nature wove and fantasy embroidered.

—*Voltaire*

THE HERITAGE BOOK

Two of my great grandsons leave for summer camp this weekend. We dropped in for a visit this afternoon to wish them a good holiday.

Both boys are very excited but Geoffrey is particularly keen, as this is his first camping experience.

As I went into his room to give him a little "tuck" money for a camp treat I saw that he was very engrossed at his desk, writing furiously.

Sheepishly he beckoned me over. "Don't tell, Gramma, but I'm writing letters to Mom and Dad. You see, Mickey told me about all the great things that we do at camp. I'm afraid I'll get so busy that I won't have time to write. I don't want Mom and Dad to worry about me so these are my "emergency" letters. If I get too busy to write I'll mail one of these prewritten ones. They just say that I'm having fun, I'm very busy, I love them and I'll see them soon."

I thought it was an ingenious idea!

SATURDAY — JULY 14

As the twilight softly falls
O'er the old cathedral walls,
Solemn peals the evening hymn!
Those sweet tones, 'mid shadows dim,
Speak of heaven-born peace to me,
Such as I would wish for thee!

SUNDAY — JULY 15

I am the vine, and you are the branches. He who dwells in me, as I dwell in him, bears much fruit, for apart from me you can do nothing.

—John 15: 5

MONDAY — JULY 16

YOUTH is happy because it has the ability to see beauty. Anyone who keeps the ability to see beauty never grows old.

—Franz Kafka

TUESDAY — JULY 17

PERHAPS it was the heat or perhaps I was overtired but today I had a headache. As one who rarely suffers from this malady I found myself feeling quite miserable.

After several aspirins and a sleep I felt considerably better. But I found myself feeling great pity for those people who suffer from repeated headaches, and in particular those who suffer from migraine headaches. I can only imagine how awful a migraine must make one feel.

Bruce came in this afternoon and, with hopes of cheering me, gave me a list of several folk remedies for the headache.

• Put leeches on your forehead.

• Apply a bag of hot cornmeal to your head.

• Soak your feet in hot water to draw the blood from your head.

• Wrap damp cloths around your head and burn scented wood (2000 B.C.).

• Lean your head against a tree and have someone drive a nail into the opposite side of the tree.

Personally I think I prefer aspirin and sleep.

THE HERITAGE BOOK

As a youngster my brother Ben was always in a hurry to get things done. He often turned in school projects that were less than his best effort. My father had a story he told in the hope of inspiring Ben to better efforts. I remember it still.

When the Athenian sculptor Phidias was carving the statue of Athena to be placed in the Acropolis he spent considerable time working on the back of the head. He was careful to carve each strand of hair so that it stood out as far as possible.

Someone watching remarked, "That figure will stand a hundred feet high, with its back to the marble wall. Who will ever know what details you are putting behind there?"

The sculptor replied, "I will know," and he continued with his detailed chiselling.

One can give another no greater gift than hope.

—Anne Warren

FRIDAY — JULY 20

JAKE Frampton gave me an amusing definition of an "old-timer": A person who remembers when people stopped spending when they ran out of money.

SATURDAY — JULY 21

TAKE time to think, it is the source of power;
Take time to play, it is the secret of perpetual youth;
Take time to laugh, it is the music of the soul;
Take time to love and be loved, it is a God-given privilege.

SUNDAY — JULY 22

FOR flowers that bloom about our feet,
For tender grass so fresh and sweet
For song of bird and hum of bee
For all things fair we hear and see
Father in heaven we thank Thee!
                    —*Ralph Waldo Emerson*

MONDAY — JULY 23

TODAY is the anniversary of Marg and Bruce's wedding day. Bruce paid Marg a most lovely compliment today; I know that he wouldn't mind me sharing it with you.

"You know, Mother, that Marg and I have had a most happy marriage. I have seen good friends whose marriages have been strained or even broken, and I have often wondered why ours has been so strong. I believe the reason lies with Marg. She is such a loving and caring person, and puts so much of herself into making our life happy. She has always been my best friend."

TUESDAY — JULY 24

A friend may well be reckoned the masterpiece of nature.

—*Ralph Waldo Emerson*

WEDNESDY — JULY 25

THOSE who dream by day are cognizant of many things which escape those who dream only by night.

—*Edgar Allan Poe*

Thursday — July 26

Rain in Summer

How beautiful is the rain!
After the dust and heat,
In the broad and fiery street,
In the narrow lane,
How beautiful is the rain!

How it clatters along the roofs,
Like the tramp of hoofs!
How it gushes and struggles out
From the throat of the overflowing spout!
Across the window-pane
It pours and pours;

And swift and wide,
With a muddy tide,
Like a river down the gutter roars
The rain, the welcome rain!
—Henry Wadsworth Longfellow

Friday — July 27

Almost everyone intends to accomplish something worthwhile—as soon as there is time.

SATURDAY — JULY 28

CONSIDER how hard it is to change yourself and you'll understand what little chance you have of trying to change others.

SUNDAY — JULY 29

AS long as the earth endures, seed time and harvest, cold and heat, summer and winter, day and night will never cease.

—Genesis 8: 22

MONDAY — JULY 30

IT'S a funny thing about life; if you refuse to accept anything but the best, you very often get it.

—W. Somerset Maugham

TUESDAY — JULY 31

ONE of my favourite summer pastimes is reading outside in the garden. I take my lawn chair right down to the back of the yard near the flower garden, and there I sit by the hour with some of my favourite books.

Many of the flowers in our garden attract a large variety of butterflies. By strange coincidence, I happened to be reading about Sir Winston Churchill today and was very surprised to learn that he was an avid butterfly fancier.

It was said that Sir Winston set aside a sizeable portion of his gardens at Chartwell for their attraction. He converted a summer house into an "emerging" area where he would sit and watch the chrysalises open and the butterflies come out. For garden parties he was known to purchase extra butterflies from a breeder.

I spent several happy hours watching the monarch butterflies flit from flower to flower. It is a most pleasant way to pass a summer's afternoon.

August

THE song that is old, but that once he loved
Somewhere in the long ago,
Means more to the singer than newer songs
With all of their fire and glow.

The valueless gift in the attic trunk,
Though romance and youth be lost,
Means more to the person who put it there
Than treasures of higher cost.

The love that has lasted through years of pain,
Though wounded and worn and old,
Contains more of heaven than younger loves,
Without the stern test, can hold.

The song and the gift that are cherished so,
And love that through time endures
Mean more in the end, when the sun is low,
Than all of life's bright new lures.

—Mary Frances Edwards

THE HERITAGE BOOK

My daughter Julia recently returned from a business trip to West Germany. While in an Islamic temple in Heidelberg she found the following inscriptions on the pillars.

Without hope you achieve nothing.

Only the foolish man regards a warning as hostility.

Acquire gold as much as you need, and wisdom as much as you can.

Loneliness is better than bad company.

Envy never rests.

For the sake of the rose one puts up with the thorn.

FRIDAY — AUGUST 3

What people say behind your back is your standing in the community.
                                                    —*Edgar Howe*

THE HERITAGE BOOK

How pleased I am to be back in Muskoka visiting with my dear friend Eleanor. Each year I look forward with eager anticipation to the time we spend together in this beautiful area of Ontario.

Eleanor's cottage is one of those large old homes built at the turn of the century. It has bright, airy bedrooms, a country-sized living room and kitchen and, loveliest of all, an enormous screened-in porch that runs across the entire front of the cottage.

Each morning Eleanor and I enjoy our tea as we look out at the lake and the boats that pass by. At an early hour the steamship "Segwun" sails past with its many passengers leaning on its polished rails, enjoying their view of the Muskoka landscape.

Often in the early morning the little girls from the cottage next door will slip over to join us for tea. We enjoy this time with the youngsters and they seem to enjoy our company as well.

All in all, Muskoka is a place that gives me great pleasure.

THE HERITAGE BOOK

SUNDAY — AUGUST 5

THE Lord is near, have no anxiety; but in everything make your requests known to God in prayer and petition with thanksgiving.
—*Philippians 4: 6*

MONDAY — AUGUST 6

NO one should make such thorough preparations for the rainy days that he cannot enjoy today's sunshine.

TUESDAY — AUGUST 7

As Eleanor and I enjoyed a lovely walk in the woods today I was reminded of Thoreau's thoughts.

"If a man walk in the woods for love of them half of each day, he is in danger of being regarded as a loafer; but if he spends his whole day as a speculator, shearing off these woods and making earth bald before her time, he is esteemed an industrious and enterprising citizen."

WEDNESDAY — AUGUST 8

RELIGION should be a steering wheel, not a spare tire.

THURSDY — AUGUST 9

NEVER fear shadows. They simply mean there's a light shining somewhere nearby.
—*Ruth Renkel*

FRIDAY — AUGUST 10

ON this day in 1876, the world's first long-distance phone call took place when Alexander Graham Bell sent the message, "To be or not to be" across eight miles of telephone wire.

Bell had set up a receiver in a footwear store in Paris, Ontario, and a transmitter in the Bell family home in Brantford. It was the first step in a communication explosion that would later disturb Bell. He used to stuff a towel around his telephone before working, exclaiming, "Now a man can think!"

THE HERITAGE BOOK

I'M always cheered when I hear stories with happy endings. This particular story took place in a large city in southern Ontario but it is one that might have been repeated anywhere.

A young boy from a poor family was the proud owner of a new bicycle. His parents had saved the money over a two-year period so that the lad might have the bicycle as a thirteenth birthday gift.

Johnny was extremely proud of his bike, keeping it meticulously clean and always locking it carefully wherever he went.

On a Friday night, as he pedalled home from his baseball game, he witnessed a car accident in which several people were injured. Dropping his bicycle he ran to offer what help he could until the police and ambulance arrived. When the ambulance left Johnny went to retrieve his bicycle only to find, to his horror, that it was missing. The devastated lad was in tears.

The policeman who drove him home felt so badly that he went immediately to his station and took up a collection. Saturday morning he delivered a brand new bicycle to the startled but ecstatic Johnny.

THE HERITAGE BOOK

SUNDAY — AUGUST 12

GLORY to Thee who safe has kept
And hast refreshed me whilst I slept;
Grant, Lord, when I from death shall wake,
I may of endless light partake.

—Bishop Thomas Ken

MONDAY — AUGUST 13

I am home again after two lovely weeks in Muskoka. I enjoyed every minute of my time in the north but I am pleased to be home again. There is something quite wonderful about that place we call "home."

Will Carleton put it quite well in these lines:

If there's a heaven upon this earth,
A fellow knows it when
He's been away from home a week,
And then gets back again.

THE HERITAGE BOOK

WHILE I was in Muskoka Bruce and Marg spent several lovely days in Quebec City. Quebec is a city that I have always loved, so I enjoyed hearing the details of their trip.

They stayed in the "Chateau Frontenac," a spectacularly beautiful old hotel that looks over the St. Lawrence River to the town of Lévis.

They did the usual tourist travels in the city, visiting the Plains of Abraham and the nearby museums. As well, they walked down the Rue du Trésor, an alley packed with open-air art stalls, and down the Côte de la Montagne, where they found Galérie Zanetlin, and Galérie Madeleine Lacerte on Côte Dinan. Lower town, or Basse-ville, provided hours of browsing in the small boutiques.

Marg, who has taken conversational French courses for several years, used her acquired language to ask natives of the city where they would choose to eat. As a result, the highlight of their trip was the wonderful dinners they ate at small, truly "French" restaurants that were unlisted in any guide book.

It was a memorable trip.

THE HERITAGE BOOK

WEDNESDAY — AUGUST 15

OH I think to step ashore
And find it Heaven;
To clasp a hand outstretched
And find it God's hand!
To breathe new air,
And that celestial air;
To feel refreshed
And find it immortality;
Ah, think to step from storm and stress
To one unbroken calm;
To awake and find it Home.

—Robert Selle

THURSDAY — AUGUST 16

THOSE who are not touched by music, I hold
to be like sticks and stones.

—Martin Luther

FRIDAY — AUGUST 17

WHY, when we are so amply provided with
words of praise, do we spend them in
such miserly fashion?

THE HERITAGE BOOK

IN the summer of 1949, Dr. J.R.P. Sclater, a minister who was visiting in Scotland, passed away. For twenty-five years Dr. Sclater, a dear friend of my husband George, had been a wonderful pastor in Toronto. He was a man of vision and influence and at his death the city newspapers carried many tributes to his character and his accomplishments.

I clipped these tributes from the newspapers to save in remembrance. I would like to share with you the words of one of Dr. Sclater's parishioners, a hospital patient whose tribute I found especially moving.

"His visits strengthened my faith. He gave me back my courage and the will to go on.

"Someday—it may be soon—I shall meet my friend again. He will look just the same, smiling and radiant as the saints at rest. 'Come in', he will say. 'I have been looking for you. We have work for you'. And I, young and strong again, will take up the humble task allotted to me."

THE HERITAGE BOOK

A Prayer in Time of Distress

HELPER of the helpless, do not hide your face from the trouble of your people. Give them strength and comfort in times of affliction, that we may proclaim the joyous news of freedom in Jesus Christ our Saviour. Amen.

LIES are easy to believe if they are what you wish were true.

—*Will Wright*

THE golden sun sinks in the west,
Retiring to his well-won rest,
Oh, may his beams from day to day
Illume with happiness thy way,
Until his last ray gleams for thee
To light thee to Eternity!

WEDNESDAY — AUGUST 22

OUR street is very quiet these days; many of the children are away at summer camp or with family or friends at cottages. I'm sure this is the same where many of you live as well.

If I may offer a suggestion, why not remember these grandchildren, nieces, nephews, or even neighbourhood children by writing a small card or letter? Children welcome mail at camp and on occasion a letter may relieve homesickness and make their stay more enjoyable.

I sent a very short letter, in which I had enclosed several cartoons, to a young neighbour who was at camp in July. He stopped in after his return to tell me how much he enjoyed his letter and how his friends had taped the cartoons to their cabin wall.

It takes so little time but it can mean so much.

THURSDY — AUGUST 23

WHEN all is said and nothing done, the committee meeting is over.

FRIDAY — AUGUST 24

I enjoyed Bruce's definition of golf: "An inef-fectual attempt to direct an uncontrollable sphere into an inaccessible hole with instruments ill-adapted to the purpose."

SATURDAY — AUGUST 25

ON this weekend several years ago I was lucky enough to attend the Canadian National Waterski Championships held at "Skier's Place" just north of Orangeville. I went with Jake Frampton and his friend Al Picard.

Al's children were skiing in the five-person pyramid formation. Unfortunately only John, Christy, and Jamie were a part of this wonderful show. The fourth child, daughter Kelly, broke her nose in a ski accident the day before the event was to begin.

I was truly amazed at what these young people are able to do on water skis. They perform slalom, jumping, and figure-skiing (or tricks) with such skill that I was in constant awe of their performances.

I hope to be able to attend another such competition in the near future.

SUNDAY — AUGUST 26

THE race is not to the swift, nor the battle to the strong, neither yet bread to the wise, nor yet riches to men of understanding, nor yet favour to men of skill; but time and chance happeneth to them all.

—Ecclesiastes 9: 11

MONDAY — AUGUST 27

IT'S hard to imagine that this is the last week of August. Although we have had some of the unmistakable signs—the shortening of our days, the slight chill of the evening air—it hardly seems possible that we are heading towards autumn.

I confess that I enjoy very much the leisure pace of summer. I like long evening walks without having to bundle up in boots or coats. I love eating outdoors in the garden. I adore iced tea and lemonade. The thought that these are passing quickly by makes me realize that I must enjoy them to the full now.

THE HERITAGE BOOK

I cannot sing the old songs
I sang long years ago,
For heart and voice would fail me,
And foolish tears would flow;
For bygone hours come o'er my heart
With each familiar strain.
I cannot sing the old songs,
Or dream those dreams again.

I cannot sing the old songs,
Their charm so sad and deep;
Their melodies would waken
Old sorrows from their sleep.
And though all unforgotten still,
And sadly sweet they be,
I cannot sing the old songs,
They are too dear to me!

I cannot sing the old songs,
For visions come again
Of golden dreams departed
And years of weary pain;
Perhaps when earthly fetters shall
Have set my spirit free
My voice shall know the old songs
For all eternity.

      —Charlotte Alington Barnard ("Claribel")

WEDNESDAY — AUGUST 29

THE Canadian Broadcasting Corporation once brought reporter d'Arce Fardy from St. John's to "correct" his distinctive Newfoundland accent. A week later, according to journalist Charles Lynch, most employees in the Corporation's speech department were "talkin' pure Newf, b'y."

THURSDAY — AUGUST 30

A woman never admits she has lost an argument. She just thinks she has failed to make her position clear.

FRIDAY — AUGUST 31

BRINGING up children is the art of hoping they'll turn out all right when they get older.

September

THE following lines bring so clearly to mind the beauty of the coming fall.

I saw old Autumn in the misty morn
Stand shadowless like silence, listening
To silence.

—Thomas Hood

The long sobbings
Of the violins
Of autumn
Wound my heart
With monotonous
Languor.

—Paul Verlaine

No spring, nor summer beauty hath such grace,
As I have seen in one autumnal face.

—John Donne

THE HERITAGE BOOK

PRAISE be to the God and Father of our Lord Jesus Christ, who has bestowed on us in Christ every spiritual blessing in the heavenly realms.

—Ephesians 1: 3

MONDAY — SEPTEMBER 3

THE hills have been high for man's mounting
The woods have been dense for his axe,
The stars have been thick for his counting
The sands have been wide for his tracks,
The sea has been deep for his diving
The poles have been broad for his sway,
But bravely he's proved in his striving
That "Where there's a will there's a way."

Should ye see, afar off, that worth winning,
Set out on the journey with trust;
And ne'er heed if your path at beginning
Should be among brambles and dust.
Though it is but by footsteps ye do it,
And hardships may hinder and stay;
Walk with faith, and be sure you'll get through
   it;
For "Where there's a will there's a way."

—Eliza Cook

THE HERITAGE BOOK

FOR most children in our area this is the first day of the new school year.

I never cease to be amazed by the enormous changes that have taken place in the education system over the past fifty years. Yet in spite of this I believe that parents' expectations have changed very little. Parents still want the best possible education for their children.

As proof of this I would like to quote from an advertisement in the July 1, 1916 edition of Funk and Wagnall's "The Literary Digest."

Wallcourt—Miss Goldsmith's School for Girls.

Wallcourt has a picturesque and healthful location in the home of Wells College, surrounded by the beautiful, historic county of Lake Cayuga. Its college preparation certificate admits to Wells, Wellesley, Vassar, Smith, and Mt. Holyoke. General academic courses, special courses in music, physical training, voice culture, interpretive and folk dancing. Home economics, swimming, horseback riding, and other healthful sports are enjoyed. Numbers are limited. References are required. Catalogue on request.

WEDNESDAY — SEPTEMBER 5

FROM an unknown teacher: "A hundred years from now it will not matter what my bank account was, the sort of house I lived in, or what kind of car I drove. But the world may be different because I was important in the life of a child."

THURSDAY — SEPTEMBER 6

THE spirit of fall seems to have arrived in our area. The young lads on our street have been outside tossing a football back and forth.

I have always enjoyed watching football and my husband George and I often attended local games to cheer our favourites. One of George's favourite football quotations was from Normie Kwong of the Edmonton Eskimos, Grey Cup champions in three consecutive years from 1954 to 1956.

The team had an unusual combination of racially mixed ball carriers. There was a white halfback from Tennessee, a black from North Carolina, and a Chinese Canadian, Normie Kwong. Kwong attributed the team's great success to the combination of "cheap American labour and Oriental ingenuity."

FRIDAY — SEPTEMBER 7

ONLY the person who has faith in himself is able to be faithful to others.

—*Erich Fromm*

SATURDAY — SEPTEMBER 8

BEGIN the day with friendliness.
Keep friendly all day long.
Keep in your soul a friendly thought—
In your heart a friendly song.
Have in your mind a word of cheer
For all who come your way,
And they will greet you too, in turn—
And wish you a happy day.

SUNDAY — SEPTEMBER 9

PRAY that the God of our Lord Jesus Christ the all glorious Father, may give you the spiritual powers of wisdom and vision.

—*Ephesians 1: 17*

THE HERITAGE BOOK

MY grandson Marshall, an avid baseball fan, loves interesting baseball stories. Here is one of his favourites.

When Bill Veeck was the president of the Chicago White Sox he created a new scoreboard. It looked like a normal scoreboard until a Chicago player hit a home run.

As the ball soared out of sight coloured fireworks flew out of the top of the scoreboard in a loud and dazzling display. As if this were not enough, coloured lights played up and down the sides of the board while horns honked, whistles tooted, and sirens screamed.

All of this happened only when Chicago scored. Casey Stengel, then manager of the New York Yankees, finally struck back. During a night game one of the Yankees hit a home run. The scoreboard remained silent. At a nod from Stengel the entire Yankee team marched onto the field in front of the dugout and turned to face the crowd. On a further signal from Stengel every player pulled out a sparkler, lighted it, and waved it enthusiastically at the silent crowd.

THE HERITAGE BOOK

FRIENDS of mine recently returned from three months in Guatemala. No, they were not on an extended holiday. Rather they were members of a group from the Canadian Executive Service Organization (C.E.S.O.), helping out in the technical area of a cable company in this third world country.

C.E.S.O. offers to third world countries the skills of well-qualified, active, recently retired Canadian men and women. These people act as advisers, helping organizations to expand their problem-solving capabilities.

As consultants they receive no salary. But they are given travel documents, visas, and information about the country where they will be sent. As well, C.E.S.O. pays economy fare to and from the projects. The client normally covers the cost of their food, accommodation, and other expenses.

"Even though we're retired, we are still useful. Working and helping people keeps us young. It's no good to be retired with nothing to do. One of our friends recently lost his wife of forty-one years. For months he was at a loss —his world was upside down. He just returned from Sri Lanka and he feels useful and alive again."

THE HERITAGE BOOK

<u>WEDNESDAY — SEPTEMBER 12</u>

ONE of the greatest weaknesses of those persons who suffer misfortune through their own fault is that they almost always try to find excuses before looking for remedies; as a result they often find remedies too late.

—Cardinal de Retz

<u>THURSDAY — SEPTEMBER 13</u>

IT has been said that a politician is the only acrobat who can open his mouth and put his foot in it while straddling the fence.

<u>FRIDAY — SEPTEMBER 14</u>

EVERY man has three characters—that which he exhibits, that which he has and that which he thinks he has.

—Alphonse Karr

SATURDAY — SEPTEMBER 15

BECAUSE you have been a friend in quiet ways

Because you have brought gleams of hope on anxious days,

Because you had time to listen when I poured out all my woe,

Because you had troubles of your own and never let them show,

Because you could still be cheerful in a world of hate and noise,

Because you remembered little things and shared your joys,

Because in the rough, tough game of life you kept your head held high,

You made me rich in a thousand things that money will never buy.

SUNDAY — SEPTEMBER 16

I pray that the eyes of your heart may be enlightened, so that you may know what is the hope of His calling, what are the riches of the glory of His inheritance in the saints.

—*Ephesians 1: 18*

THE HERITAGE BOOK

IT is better to say "thank you" and not mean it, than to mean it and not say it.

A lot of good could be accomplished if nobody cared who got the credit.

THE man who never makes mistakes loses a great many chances to learn something.

IT isn't necessary to blow out the other person's light to let your own shine.

THE HERITAGE BOOK

THIS was an extremely exciting day for my granddaughter Phyllis and her husband Bill. Their children, Justin and Jenny, spent their first day in kindergarten.

While the children in the other grades are into their third week of class, the students in the kindergarten have had only home visits from their teachers. As well, they have had staggered start times. All of this is meant to make their first experience at school an easier adjustment for them.

Fortunately, Justin and Jenny were both very pleased with their new teacher and most anxious to start "real school" (after their year in nursery school).

I think Phyllis had the most difficult morning. "You know, Gram, it seems like only yesterday they were tiny newborns, and now five years have flown by and they're happily walking away from me to face a whole new part of their lives."

Although it is difficult to see one's children leave for school I feel that Phyllis and Bill should be proud to have raised children who are happy and well adjusted enough to accept school so easily.

THE HERITAGE BOOK

THIS evening Marg, Bruce, some of our neighbours, and I had a most enjoyable time playing Monopoly. I was intrigued to hear how the game, enjoyed by many millions of people, came to be.

Back in 1932, a man by the name of Charles Darrow was out of a job and broke. His wife was expecting a baby. He was a heating engineer, but there were no jobs available and Darrow and his wife were just barely subsisting on the few odd jobs he could get as a handyman. Things were bleak.

In the evenings, to take their minds off their troubles, Darrow and his wife made up a little game in which they could pretend they were millionaires. Recalling pleasant vacations in nearby Atlantic City, they reconstructed the area adjoining the boardwalk. Darrow carved houses and hotels out of small pieces of wood. They called the game "Monopoly."

The couple introduced the game to their friends and, three years later, the game was being marketed nationally by Parker Brothers. Darrow and his wife became millionaires.

Sunday — September 23

BE generous to one another, tender-hearted, forgiving one another as God in Christ forgave you.

—Ephesians 4: 32

Monday — September 24

"NECESSITY may be the mother of invention, but frustration is often the father of success."

Murray Spangler, a store janitor in Canton, Ohio, could attest to this philosophy. Spangler, who swept floors, was frustrated that the dust made him wheeze and cough. Many men would have given up and quit. Instead Spangler set out to find a better way to clean floors. Could the broom be eliminated? Perhaps something that would suck up the dust? This idea led to a crude but workable vacuum cleaner.

Spangler introduced this machine to an old friend who owned a leather business, in the hope that he would finance it for him. His friend's name was H. W. Hoover.

THE HERITAGE BOOK

RETENTIVE memory may be a good thing but the ability to forget is the true token of greatness.

As I sit beside my window
Buried deep in troubled thought,
The beauty spread before me
Brings the comfort I have sought.

For up along the hilltop
Where pines are darkest green,
A single drop of colour
In a scarlet tree is seen.

Oh, who can doubt that God above
His vigilance has kept,
Who caused the very hills to glow
With colour while we slept.

A token of His handiwork
Is seen in every tree,
When nature hangs new pictures
For all the world to see.

—Frances C. Cowles

THE HERITAGE BOOK

SYMPATHY is the first great lesson which man should learn. Unless he learns to feel for things in which he has no personal interest, he can achieve nothing generous or noble.

—Sir Thomas Talfourd

MY good friends Will and Muriel stopped by for a visit. Will, a wonderful gardener, is reaping the last of his vegetables from what was a "bumper crop" this summer.

I really like to listen to Will talk about his garden. His obvious pleasure in it is so wonderful to witness. I feel good just seeing his joy in the results of his hard work and effort.

That kind of person is a great spirit booster and a happy type to have around.

PATTING children on their heads will never stunt their growth.

THE HERITAGE BOOK

SET your mind on God's kingdom and his justice before everything else, and all the rest will come to you as well. So do not be anxious about tomorrow, tomorrow will look after itself. Each day has troubles enough of its own.

—*Matthew 6: 33-34*

October

What are the things I love to see
In autumn when the year grows old?
The black gum leaves of scarlet red;
A hillside poplar turned to gold.

What are the things I love to hear
In autumn when the year is spent?
The wild geese flying overhead,
And drowsy rain with its clean scent.

What are the things I love to smell
In autumn when the year is done?
Blue curling smoke from burning leaves,
And wild grapes purpling in the sun.

Ah, autumn in her passing, leaves
The memory of a lovely song,
And for the heart a legacy
That will last all the winter long.

—*William Arnette Wooford*

THE HERITAGE BOOK

Tuesday — October 2

THE great French general, Charles de Gaulle, had a daughter, Anne, who was mentally retarded. The general loved her dearly and spent many happy hours with her. He never stopped hoping, however, that Anne might someday be as other children. It was a frequent and fervent prayer from both de Gaulle and his wife.

Sadly, Anne died at the age of twenty. As de Gaulle stood crying at the gravesite he turned to his wife and said, "Now, at last, Anne is like all the other children here."

Wednesday — October 3

THE greatest pleasure I know is to do good by stealth and have it found out by accident.

—Charles Lamb

Thursday — October 4

IF you wonder what the world is coming to, remember: so did your grandfather.

THE HERITAGE BOOK

My granddaughter Phyllis' best friend, Christie, is a schoolteacher. She has followed in a long family tradition—her mother, grandmother, and great grandmother were all teachers.

Christie recently shared with me an old letter she had found in a scrapbook belonging to her great grandmother. This letter had come from the school board at the time of her hiring. It listed the rules that were to be obeyed should she accept the position in the school.

1. You will not marry during the term of your contract.
2. You are not to keep company with men.
3. You must be home between the hours of 8 p.m. and 6 a.m.
4. You may not loiter downtown in ice cream stores.
5. You may not smoke cigarettes.
6. You may not dress in bright colours.
7. You may not dye your hair.
8. You must wear at least two petticoats.
9. Your dresses must not be more than two inches above the ankle.
10. Your schoolroom floors must be swept daily, washed weekly, and the fire started at 7 a.m. so the room will be warm by 8.

THE HERITAGE BOOK

MANY years ago Alberta experienced an unusually cold and wet summer. September was only slightly better, but October finally brought warm, sunny days.

A gentleman heading for the country stopped to service his car. He felt compelled to comment on the fine day to the young native lad who was filling his gas tank.

"Sure is a great Indian summer we're having."

The native replied, "It sure beats the white man's summer we had earlier."

Thanksgiving Sunday

CREATOR of the fruitful earth you made us stewards of all things. Give us grateful hearts for all your goodness and steadfast wills to use your bounty well, that the whole human family, today and in generations to come, may with us give thanks for the riches of your creation. We ask this in the name of Jesus Christ, Our Lord.

Book of Alternative Services
- Anglican Church of Canada

MONDAY — OCTOBER 8

THIS is the day that we, in Canada, celebrate the Thanksgiving holiday. Although each family celebrates in its own unique way, generally speaking this is the most family-oriented holiday next to Christmas. Possibly one of the reasons for this comes with the holiday's title. Family is one of the most important parts of our lives. If we are grateful for something good in our lives that something, very often, is our family.

We McCanns are no exception. Although we are widely scattered, nearly all of our family members make a great effort to attend the Thanksgiving family get-together.

This afternoon's meal will be delicious, as usual, but much of the happiness of this day will, for me, come from seeing the whole family enjoying this special time in each other's company.

TUESDAY — OCTOBER 9

FORTY is the old age of youth; fifty is the youth of old age.

—*Victor Hugo*

THE HERITAGE BOOK

Wednesday — October 10

Theodore Quinn writes, "They had a tranquillizer back in my grandfather's day. It practically guaranteed you a good night's sleep. It was called hard work."

Thursday — October 11

The most wonderful of all things in life, I believe, is the discovery of another human being with whom one's relationship has a growing depth, beauty and joy as the years increase. This inner progressiveness of love between two human beings is a most marvellous thing. It cannot be found by looking for it or by passionately wishing for it. It is sort of a divine accident.

—*Sir Hugh Walpole*

Friday — October 12

Strangers show up when they need you—friends when you need them.

THE HERITAGE BOOK

WEATHER, it seems, is a topic of conversation at all times of the year. Today I offer you just a few of the many "forecasts" that are given to us in rhyme.

Rain before seven,
Fair by eleven.

A sunshiny shower,
Won't last half an hour.

The South wind brings wet weather,
The North wind wet and cold together;
The West wind always brings us rain,
The East wind blows it back again.

Rainbow at night—sailors' delight.
Rainbow at morning—sailors take warning.

If bees stay at home, rain will soon come;
If they fly away, fine will be the day.

Evening red and morning grey
Set the traveller on his way;
But evening grey and morning red
Bring the rain upon his head.

THE HERITAGE BOOK

A word softly spoken is like apples of gold in settings of silver.

—*Proverbs 25: 11*

THIS past weekend was spent doing up our jars of tomatoes, chili, and spaghetti sauces.

Did you know that the tomato originated in wild forms found in the Andes of South America? Migrating Indians brought it north into Central America. Mexico's Aztec and Mayan Indians cultivated xitomatle, later called tomatl or tomati, which gave the fruit its name.

In the early sixteenth century the Spanish conquistadors brought the tomato to Europe. It was quickly accepted in Spain and Italy, and in sixteenth-century England it was grown as an ornamental plant. Colonists carried the tomato to North America. It didn't appear in Canadian seed catalogues or gardens until the early nineteenth century.

Canadians now spend nearly half a billion dollars a year on tomatoes. Food for thought?

<u>TUESDAY — OCTOBER 16</u>

IF I had to choose between beauty and truth, I should not hesitate; it is beauty that I should keep, feeling sure that it bears within it a truth loftier and more profound than truth itself.

—Anatole France

<u>WEDNESDAY — OCTOBER 17</u>

OF course there's a devil. Who do you think tickles your nose as soon as your arms are full of packages?

<u>THURSDAY — OCTOBER 18</u>

REMEMBER that happiness is as contagious as gloom. It should be the duty of those who are happy to let others know of their gladness.

THE HERITAGE BOOK

IN the month of October there is a unique festival in the state of Tennessee. It is the National Storytelling Festival, held annually in Jonesborough, a little town in the Appalachian mountains of East Tennessee.

Thousands come to hear and hundreds come to tell tales—African, Indian, and Scottish stories, mountain yarns, legends, myths, folk and fairy tales, tales with tricks, morals, humour, and the most popular of all—ghost stories.

The ghost stories are told Saturday night around a bonfire at the edge of the cemetery. With the graves casting shadows on the dark figures, listeners sit captivated as, one by one, storytellers relate their hair-raising tales.

The Swappin' Ground is a popular storytelling arena where anyone can get an audience. The stage is fresh-cut grass bordered by logs and bales of hay. Storytellers simply sign in on a sheet posted to a tree. You get ten minutes to tell your best tale to an audience eager to appreciate.

Stories are a magnificent form of entertainment, and visitors at this festival can enjoy three days of the best storytelling imaginable.

SATURDAY — OCTOBER 20

I remember my youth and the feeling that I will never come back anymore—the feeling that I could last forever, outlast the sea, the earth, and all men.

—Joseph Conrad

SUNDAY — OCTOBER 21

AFTER breakfast Jesus said to Simon Peter, "Simon, son of Jonah, do you love me more than all else?"

"Yes, Lord," he answered, "you know that I love you."

"Then feed my lambs," he said.

—John 21: 15

MONDAY — OCTOBER 22

THERE is no witness so terrible—no accuser so powerful as conscience which dwells within us.

—Sophocles

THE HERITAGE BOOK

As evening shadows gently fall
On a crisp October day,
We gaze with open wonder
On nature's glorious display.

The leaves have changed their colour
Now that summer's bid goodbye,
And the beauty of a rainbow
Can be seen through forest high.

It's been man's fondest ambition
To portray in colours bright
The glory of Dame Nature
On a crisp October night.

Yet paint and brush or even words
And all the skill that's good,
Can never paint the beauty
Of an autumn-tinted wood.

—*William Knowles*

WEDNESDAY — OCTOBER 24

THERE is much truth in this proverb passed
along to me by our mailman.

"You'll have a better life if you make the
most of the best and the least of the worst."

Thursday — October 25

My son-in-law John related this little anecdote to me. As a clergyman he found it most amusing.

Several playmates found a dead squirrel and, feeling that a proper burial was in order, they placed the deceased in a shoe box and dug a hole.

The minister's young son, a member of the funeral party, was called upon to perform the prayer.

With the proper solemn voice he repeated his version of the prayer for the dead. "Glory be to the Faaatherr and unto the Sonnn and into the hole you gooo."

Friday — October 26

Two things fill my mind with ever-increasing wonder and awe, the more often and the more intensely the reflection dwells on them: the starry heavens above me and the moral law within me.

—Immanuel Kant

THE HERITAGE BOOK

THERE are two things to aim at in life: first, to get what you want; and, after that, to enjoy it. Only the wisest of mankind achieve the second.

—Logan Pearsall Smith

I will sing to the Lord as long as I live, all my life I will sing psalms to my God. May my meditation please the Lord and I show my joy in him. Bless the Lord, my soul, O praise the Lord.

—Psalm 104: 33-35

THE HERITAGE BOOK

<u>MONDAY — OCTOBER 29</u>

IF you want to feel rich, just count all of the things you have that money can't buy.

<u>TUESDAY — OCTOBER 30</u>

WE spent a most pleasant evening with Phyllis, Bill, and the twins. After dinner we helped the children carve their pumpkins.

Although Jenny and Justin have "trick-or-treated" for several years, this is the first time they have really understood the fun of Halloween and wanted their own pumpkins.

I really enjoyed seeing the two pumpkin characters emerge. Jenny's jack-o'-lantern is happy-faced and non-threatening. Justin's, on the other hand, is as fierce as a pumpkin could possibly look.

It really is fun to participate in the joys of childhood.

<u>WEDNESDAY — OCTOBER 31</u>

FROM ghoulies and ghosties and
long-leggety beasties
And things that go bump in the night,
Good Lord, deliver us!

November

All Saints Day

Comfort one another
For the way is often dreary
And the feet are often weary
And the heart is very sad.
There is heavy burden-bearing
When it seems that none are caring
And we half-forget that we were ever glad.

Comfort one another
With the hand-clasp close and tender,
With the sweetness love can render
And the looks of friendly eyes.
Do not wait with words unspoken
While life's daily bread is broken —
Gentle speech is oft like manna from the skies.
                                            —*Margaret E. Sangster*

Perhaps the closest we can come to being a "saint" here on this earth is to be a good friend.

Friday — November 2

EACH year I am amazed at how quickly October becomes November. By that I mean that somehow we go from trees with exquisitely coloured leaves to trees that are trunks and branches only. The change is so complete and happens so quickly—and suddenly it's November.

Although each month has its own particular beauty one certainly needs to search for magnificence in November. I did find something, however.

Now that the trees are bare it is very easy to see the squirrels as they fly from branch to branch, chasing one another as children would in a game of tag. Indeed, I became so engrossed this morning that nearly two hours passed as I sat, mesmerized, at the window.

Ah, November.

Saturday — November 3

COMPROMISE is the art of cutting a cake so that everybody believes he or she got the biggest piece.

THE HERITAGE BOOK

SUNDAY — NOVEMBER 4

MOST merciful Father, who hast been pleased to receive unto thyself our brethren departed: Grant to us who are still in our pilgrimage and who walk as yet by faith, that having served Thee faithfully in this world, we may with all Christian souls, be joined hereafter to the company of thy blessed saints in glory. Amen.

—Book of Common Prayer

MONDAY — NOVEMBER 5

SOMEONE who daydreams about losing weight is wishful shrinking.

TUESDAY — NOVEMBER 6

ONE of the great joys of my life is my music. As my former readers know, I decided only a few years ago to take piano lessons. It was something I had wanted to do for many years, but it was not until I asked myself one question that I decided to go ahead. I asked myself, "If I should die tomorrow, what would be one thing I wanted to do but never did?" The answer, of course, was that I wanted to take piano lessons.

I have enjoyed every minute of my lessons, the practice and, yes, my playing. Although I will never be a "Liberace" on the keys I can play with ease and pleasure.

My only regret is that I waited so long to try. If you have something that you would like to do, I urge you—go ahead—take the plunge—try it!

WEDNESDAY — NOVEMBER 7

WHEN I look back on all these worries, I remember the story of the old man who said, on his deathbed, that he had a lot of trouble in his life, most of which never happened.

—*Winston Churchill*

THE HERITAGE BOOK

<u>THURSDAY — NOVEMBER 8</u>

MOST of us are average people except to those who love us.

<u>FRIDAY — NOVEMBER 9</u>

I recently read a letter in a newspaper that touched me deeply. It was a thank-you note from the recipient of a heart transplant.

It read, in part, "I am a heart transplant recipient. Eighteen months after the surgery I am forty-one years old, healthy, happy, and leading a normal life. It is like a miracle. I feel so blessed.

"I owe this life to someone whom I never met, some healthy young person who died unexpectedly. I will be eternally grateful to the family who allowed their loved one's heart to be donated.

"My message is to that unknown donor and family. There is no way I can adequately thank you. I think of you every day and pray for you every night, and I shall do so for the rest of my life."

Not one of us imagines that we shall die at an early age. How wonderful it is that so many people give others the gift of life when their own is tragically cut short.

THE HERITAGE BOOK

The Soldier

Iᶠ I should die, think only this of me:
That there's some corner of a foreign field
That is forever England. There shall be
In that rich earth a richer dust concealed;
A dust whom England bore, shaped, made
   aware,
Gave, once, her flowers to love, her ways to
   roam;
A body of England's, breathing English air,
Washed by the rivers, blest by suns of home.
And think, this heart, all evil shed away,
A pulse in the eternal mind, no less
Gives somewhere back to the thoughts by
   England given;
Her sights and sounds; dreams happy as her
   day;
And laughter, learnt of friends, and gentleness,
In hearts at peace, under an English heaven.

               —*Rupert Brookes*

Sunday — November 11

Remembrance Day

How blessed are the peace-makers: God
shall call them his sons.

               —*Matthew 5: 9*

THE HERITAGE BOOK

MONDAY — NOVEMBER 12

My good friend Marcia lives in Boston, Massachusetts. On weekends she often drives down to Cape Cod, a beautiful area on the ocean. The Cape is dotted with small towns, each of which has numerous boutiques or specialty shops.

One of Marcia's favourites is a small antique shop in Provincetown.

"What drew me to this store was the sign posted on the door to indicate hours of business. 'We are open Monday through Saturday at about 11:00 a.m. (or noon) but occasionally as early as 9:00 or 10:00. Some days we open as late as 1:00. We close at 5:30 or 6:00. If it's a nice day I might close at 4:00 or 4:30 so that I can walk on the beach. I hope this suits you. Thank you. The Management.' "

TUESDAY — NOVEMBER 13

My friend Will remarked to a neighbour that some friends were coming over to "bird-watch."

His neighbour was silent for a few moments and then said quizzically, "Watch 'em what?"

INDIAN CORN

WEDNESDAY — NOVEMBER 14

THE most creative job in the world involves taste, fashion, decorating, recreation, education, transportation, psychology, romance, cuisine, designing, literature, medicine, handicraft, art, horticulture, economics, government, community relations, pediatrics, geriatrics, entertainment, maintenance, purchasing, direct mail, law, accounting, religion, energy, and management.

Anyone who can handle all of these has to be somebody special. She is. She's a homemaker.

THURSDAY — NOVEMBER 15

A happy Thanksgiving to our friends south of the border.

For this Thanksgiving Day, O Lord,
To you our thanks we give.

FRIDAY — NOVEMBER 16

THE quickest way to make yourself feel better is to help someone who feels worse.

THE HERITAGE BOOK

EVERY parting gives a foretaste of death; every coming together again a foretaste of the resurrection.

—Arthur Schopenhauer

MAY the peace of God which passeth all understanding keep your hearts and minds in the knowledge and love of God and of his Son, Jesus Christ our Lord.

—Book of Common Prayer

As a final incentive before giving up a difficult task, try to imagine it successfully accomplished by someone you violently dislike.

LUCK is what happens when preparation meets opportunity.

WEDNESDAY — NOVEMBER 21

YOU are as young as your faith, as old as your doubt; as young as your self-confidence, as old as your fear; as young as your hope, as old as your despair.

—Samuel Ullman

THURSDAY — NOVEMBER 22

THIS is a day infamous in American history. On this date in 1963 in Dallas, Texas, President John Fitzgerald Kennedy, the 35th president of the United States, was slain.

In the years since Kennedy's death we have learned more than we ever wanted to know of his imperfections. But during the thousand days that he spent in office he seemed to imbue the country with a kind of optimism, a freshness, a yearning for action.

With his direct and vigorous speeches he made Americans feel that they were living in stirring times and that he was truly a leader, taking them to new heights.

"And so, my fellow Americans, ask not what your country can do for you; ask what you can do for your country."

Friday — November 23

SUCCESSFUL people have a knack for solving difficult problems. Often it is not possible to solve a problem the way one originally planned. At those times it is necessary to stop, re-evaluate, and come up with a different approach.

Abraham Lincoln used to tell a story about Ulysses A. Grant to illustrate this point.

When Grant was a boy he liked to attend the circus with the boys of his neighbourhood. One circus had a mule trained so that no one could ride it without being thrown. The circus offered one dollar—an enormous sum in those days—to anyone who could stay on the mule while he went around the ring.

Several men tried but were easily tossed off. At the urging of his friends Grant decided to try. He hung on gamely but slid over the mule's head as the others had done.

Grant picked himself up, thought for a few moments, and then asked for another try. This time he got on the mule facing backwards, with his feet around the animal's stomach and holding its tail fiercely. The mule tried to shed its rider—to no avail. The mule gave up and Grant collected his dollar.

THE HERITAGE BOOK

I was lucky enough to attend a hockey game at Maple Leaf Gardens recently. My grandson Marshall, an avid hockey fan, was given a pair of tickets in the "red" section of the Gardens. Knowing that I hadn't been to a game in a very long time he generously asked me to accompany him.

I loved every minute of it! The game was well played, and to the crowd's delight the Maple Leafs were winners.

I must confess, though, that I was almost more interested in the time between the hockey periods. The object of my fascination was the "Zamboni" machine. In my day the ice was flooded between periods with hoses, and later with "sophisticated" tractors pulling a water tank.

Frank Zamboni put together his first ice resurfacing machine in 1947. He used a war-surplus jeep engine, the front ends of two automobiles, a series of pulleys, and a wooden bin to catch the ice shavings.

The "Zamboni" has now progressed to amazing heights of technology and I got a "silly old lady's" thrill from watching it.

SUNDAY — NOVEMBER 25

PRAISE my soul, the King of heaven,
To His feet thy tribute bring,
Ransomed, healed, restored, forgiven,
Evermore his praises sing;
Alleluia, Alleluia,
Glorious in his faithfulness.

Angels, help us to adore Him,
Ye behold Him face to face,
Sun and moon bow down before Him;
Dwellers all in time and space,
Alleluia, Alleluia,
Praise with us the God of grace.
—*Rev. H. F. Lyte (1834)*

MONDAY — NOVEMBER 26

WISDOM is a goddess who bestows her
favours only on those who have laboured
hard to reach her throne.
—*Bern Williams*

TUESDAY — NOVEMBER 27

EACH day is an opportunity to start all over again, to cleanse our minds and hearts anew and to clarify our vision. And let us not clutter up today with the leavings of other days.

—Oliver Wendell Holmes

WEDNESDAY — NOVEMBER 28

ALTHOUGH I don't often discuss politics with my friends I do enjoy many of the popular political jokes.

Jake Frampton passed on this amusing item in the hopes that my readers might enjoy it.

A Conservative is a man who throws a twenty-five foot rope to a person drowning fifty feet from shore, and shouts encouragement for him to swim the other half for the good of his character.

A Liberal throws a fifty-foot line to a person drowning only twenty-five feet from shore—and, after throwing it, lets go of the other end, and walks away to do another good deed.

Thursday — November 29

What you can do, or dream you can, begin it: boldness has genius, power and magic in it.

—Goethe

Friday — November 30

The budget should be balanced, the treasury should be refilled, public debt should be reduced, the arrogance of officialdom should be tempered and controlled, and assistance to foreign lands should be reduced lest the state become bankrupt. The people should be forced to work and not depend on government for subsistence.

"One of our modern politicians speaking his platform," you say to yourself.

Not at all—this speech was made by Cicero (106-43 B.C.).

December

W<small>ITH</small> our brief snowfall last night came the memory of the poem "Snow Picture" by Nancy Byrd Turner.

Yesterday hills and woods were gray
And boughs were bare and brown
But all last night silently, silently
Snow came down.

All night long over the fields,
Quiet and soft and slow,
With a footprint, steadily, steadily
Walked the snow.

Now at dawn there is nothing but snow
Nothing but whiteness now
Except the flame of a redbird's wing
On a feathery bough.

THE HERITAGE BOOK

IN all this remember how critical the moment is. It is time for you to wake out of sleep, for deliverance is nearer to us than when we first believed. It is far on in the night, day is near. Let us, therefore, throw off the deeds of darkness and put on our armour of light. Let us behave with decency as befits the day.

—Romans 13: 11-13

ALTHOUGH many young women have broken the sex barrier of all-male hockey teams, in some areas it is still unusual to have girls playing on the boys' teams.

One father cautioned his daughter to expect some verbal abuse. It looked as if he was right when, following her first game, one of the opposing players skated over and whispered something into her helmeted ear.

When her father asked later what had been said, the girl blushed furiously and replied, "He said 'Good game, beautiful!' "

TUESDAY — DECEMBER 4

MY daughter Julia was visiting with us for the weekend. Julia is an executive with a large corporation and in this capacity she attends many social functions.

Julia is always very popular at parties and much of her success, I believe, has to do with the fact that she is an excellent listener. She takes time to hear what others are saying and she is genuinely interested in their ideas and opinions.

We talked about this on the weekend and Julia made an interesting observation.

"You know, Mom, there are two types of conversationalists: those who listen to what the other person has to say, and those who use the interval to plan their next remark."

This is certainly worth thinking about.

WEDNESDAY — DECEMBER 5

HAPPINESS is much more dependent on the mental attitude than on external resources. This would be an absurdly obvious platitude were it not for the fact that ninety-nine out of a hundred persons do not believe it.
—William Lyon Phelps

Thursday — December 6

Man strives for glory, honour, fame,
That all the world may know his name.
Amasses wealth by brain and hand;
Becomes a power in the land.
But when he nears the end of life
And looks back o'er the years of strife,
He finds that happiness depends
On none of these, but love of friends.

Friday — December 7

Maturity is the ability to do a job whether or not you are supervised, to carry money without spending it, and to bear an injustice without wanting to get even.

—*Ann Landers*

Saturday — December 8

The only gracious way to accept an insult is to ignore it; if you can't ignore it, top it; if you can't top it, laugh at it; if you can't laugh at it, it's probably deserved.

THE HERITAGE BOOK

AND may the God of hope fill you with all joy and peace, by your faith in Him, until by the power of the Holy Spirit, you overflow with hope.

—Romans 15: 13

MONDAY — DECEMBER 10

THIS past weekend I spent a lovely day with Fred, June, and their sons Mickey and Geoffrey. We paid a visit to Black Creek Pioneer Village in Toronto.

There never was a real Black Creek Village. What we see is a collection of buildings brought from various locations and arranged to represent a rural community just prior to Confederation.

Christmas in Black Creek reflects the different Yuletide traditions of the pioneers. In the home of the Pennsylvania Germans is a tiny tree, hung with dried apples and balls of home-dyed fleece balls. In the English Burwick House, wreaths and swags of evergreen abound on mantels and stair rails.

A sleigh ride through the village is a glorious way to see it all.

THE middle school in our area has continued a lovely Christmas tradition again this year.

In November, interested children submit their names to be "twinned" with a resident in our local nursing home. The first visit is a "get-acquainted" ice cream party at the nursing home. The students are introduced to their "twin" in a social setting. They make ice cream sundaes and spend time getting to know one another.

Early in December the children and their older companions are transported by bus to a shopping mall, where students help to do some Christmas shopping or window browsing. When they return a merry time is had wrapping parcels and singing carols.

There are several other outings, including the Christmas concert at the school, and a tour of Christmas-lit homes.

The highlight is the Christmas dinner prepared and served by the students in the week before Christmas.

It has given this holiday a wonderful new meaning for both students and seniors and I congratulate the principal for his thoughtfulness.

WEDNESDAY — DECEMBER 12

As we move ever closer to Christmas and the hustle and bustle of the season threatens to wear us down, it is important to remember why we are celebrating.

Take time to think about the child born in that humble stable so very long ago. Take time to rejoice in His birth. Don't lose sight of what Christmas means. At times it is difficult to see through the trappings of the holiday and to remember why we celebrate.

Take time.

THURSDAY — DECEMBER 13

On the morning after a snowfall a very small boy knocked on the door of a neighbour and friend, Lila McGuinness. He wanted to shovel her front walk and, after a short discussion, one dollar was the agreed price.

Shortly the bell rang again. "There are three of us and we don't know how to divide a dollar. Could you please make the price seventy-five cents instead?"

FRIDAY — DECEMBER 14

WHEN you come to the end of a perfect
day,
And you sit alone with your thought,
While the chimes ring out with a carol gay
For the joy that the day has brought,
Do you think what the end of a perfect day
Can mean to a tired heart,
When the sun goes down with a flaming ray
And the dear friends have to part.

Well this is the end of a perfect day,
Near the end of a journey too,
But it leaves a thought that is big and strong,
With a wish that is kind and true,
For mem'ry has painted this perfect day
With colours that never fade,
And we find at the end of a perfect day
The soul of a friend we've made.
—*Carrie Jacobs-Bond*

SATURDAY — DECEMBER 15

To create a housing shortage in a huge country, heavily wooded, with a small population—ah, that's proof of pure political genius.
—*Richard J. Needham*

SUNDAY — DECEMBER 16

THIS morning we sang several Christmas carols at our morning service. The carols are some of my favourite hymns, and here is a verse from one of the loveliest.

Once in Royal David's city
Stood a lowly cattle shed.
Where a mother laid her baby
In a manger for his bed
Mary was that mother mild
Jesus Christ her little child.

MONDAY — DECEMBER 17

As more and more Christmas cards arrive I am thrilled to hear from old friends and acquaintances from many parts of the world.

Cards and notes renew old friendships and buoy our spirits. It is a tradition I enjoy immensely.

TUESDAY — DECEMBER 18

PLEASE don't forget those friends and relatives who are shut-ins. At this time of year a visit, no matter how brief, can bring such pleasure to those who are unable to be out and around.

It takes so little time but can mean so much. No one wants to feel forgotten.

WEDNESDAY — DECEMBER 19

CHOOSING appropriate gifts is a difficult task. For those of us on fixed incomes it can become a truly monumental chore. In discussions with friends of similar means, several good suggestions came up and I pass them on in the hope that one or more may be of benefit to you.

When buying for more than one child in a family, a good game such as Scrabble or Monopoly can be given as a joint gift.

The gift of your time as a babysitter is a welcome one for young parents.

Jars of preserves and vegetables are enjoyed by apartment dwellers who no longer have gardens of their own.

THE HERITAGE BOOK

WE are often tempted by delicious, rich foods at this time of year. Each time I hear Bruce groan about his waistline I remember the mother of a good friend of mine. She decided that she should lose some weight and so she sent away for a diet program recommended in a magazine.

After reading it she threw it away in disgust. "For gracious sakes, girls," she said. "They try to make you cut down on food!"

TRUE happiness consists not in the multitude of friends, but in the worth and choice.
—*Ben Jonson*

FRANCIS Bacon said, "Age appears to be best in four things: old wood to burn, old wine to drink, old friends to trust, and old authors to read."

THE HERITAGE BOOK

SUNDAY — DECEMBER 23

AND the angel Gabriel said to her, "Do not be afraid, Mary: for you have found favour with God. And behold, you will conceive in your womb, and bear a son, and you shall name him Jesus. He will be great, and will be the Son of the Most High.

—Luke 1: 30-32

MONDAY — DECEMBER 24

THE Christmas Eve service was as lovely as ever. Who could not enjoy the beautiful candles, the red poinsettias, the crèche, and the children dressed as angels, singing joyfully of the Saviour's birth. It truly is a time to rejoice.

TUESDAY — DECEMBER 25

Christmas Day

JESUS Christ is born today. Alleluia.

THE HERITAGE BOOK

IT hardly seems possible that Christmas Day has come and gone.

This year our family dinner was held at the home of my grandson Fred and his family. Their house in the country made for a truly old-fashioned Christmas.

The children, of course, were most anxious to open gifts, so with help from Bruce and John (our "elves") the gifts were distributed and opened.

The "oohs" and "aahs" attested to everyone's appreciation. Fred had earlier received a video camera and he was kept busy filming the excitement.

In the early afternoon dinner was served. Huge platters of turkey and bowls of steaming mashed potatoes and turnip disappeared as if by magic.

The trifle dessert was a very popular dish with children and adults alike.

It was a wonderful day made special by the fact that all of our family was present.

THE HERITAGE BOOK

THURSDAY — DECEMBER 27

THE lovely phrase "remember when"
Sets every heart aglow,
As we drift back in memory
To the happy long ago.

FRIDAY — DECEMBER 28

My friend Marcia sent this to me from an
unknown author.

I am not a special person
I am not especially strong
I am not especially gifted
I simply do not like to show my weakness
And I hate to lose
So I am a person who tries hard
That's all there is to me.

SATURDAY — DECEMBER 29

IF you've got troubles, the best eraser in the
world is a good night's sleep.

THE HERITAGE BOOK

O God, who makest us glad with the yearly remembrance of the birth of thy only Son, Jesus Christ: Grant that as we joyfully receive him as our Redeemer, we may with sure confidence behold him when he shall come again to be our Judge; who liveth and reigneth with thee and the Holy Ghost now and ever. Amen.
                              —*The Book of Common Prayer*

O nce again we come to the end of another year. I would like to offer this message in the hopes that we may keep it in our hearts during the year to come.

"Shall the human heart live for itself; gather and store for its own good? There is no such thing as one's own good. Goodness is mutual, is communal; is only gained by giving and receiving."